THE INDEPENDENT GUIDE TO HONG KONG DISNEYLAND 2020

G. COSTA

D1602273

Limit of Liability and Disclaimer of Warranty:
The publisher has used its best efforts in preparing this book, and the information provided herein is provided "as is." Independent Guides and the author make no representation or warranties concerning the accuracy or completeness of the contents of this book and expressly disclaims any implied warranties of merchantability or fitness for any particular purpose and shall in no event be liable for any loss of profit or any other damage, including but not limited to special, incidental, consequential, or other damages.

Please read all signs before entering attractions, as well as the terms and conditions of any companies used. Prices are approximate and do fluctuate.

Note: This guide is written in British English, which is widely used throughout Hong Kong.

Contents

Hong Kong Disneyland was The Walt Disney Company's first foray into the Chinese theme park market. The theme park was built incredibly quickly with the ground-breaking ceremony in January 2003 and the park's opening in September 2005.

The theme park's main aim was to help increase Hong Kong's tourism, especially after the SARS epidemic devastated the region's economy in 2003. The park is jointly owned by The Walt Disney Company and the Government of Hong Kong.

The theme park is well-located in a lush tropical landscape unlike any other Disney park. It is well-connected to Hong Kong and is about a $200HK 25-minute taxi ride from the city centre, $100HK 10-minute ride from Hong Kong International airport, or just a $15-$20HK fare by the ubiquitous MTR train system, which drops you off directly at the resort.

Mainland China now has a bigger Disney theme park resort at Shanghai Disneyland, and the two resorts are very different. Hong Kong Disneyland is widely regarded as Disney's least-successful resort, whereas Shanghai Disneyland has been a grand success.

Hong Kong Disneyland is the second-least-visited Disney theme park in the world, after Walt Disney Studios Park in Paris, and received 6.7 million visitors in 2018 (2019's numbers are likely to be lower due to the Hong Kong city riots affecting tourism, as are 2020's number due to the global pandemic).

Outside of peak periods like Christmas and Summer, the park doesn't have the hustle and bustle of the other Disney theme parks – if you like to get on rides with shorter waits, this may well be your favourite Disney theme park! However, it is still the 16th most visited theme park in the world.

As of 2020, the resort is made up of one theme park and three resort hotels.

2020 is a big year for the resort as it celebrates its 15th anniversary – a reimagining of the park's iconic castle will be unveiled, and work continues on a new Frozen area for the park, which is set to open in 2021. This is a great time to visit!

Hong Kong Disneyland is a place where dreams really do come true for guests every single day, and you are about to become one of them.

RMB (mainland Chinese Yuan) in cash. This is not the case throughout the rest of Hong Kong, however.

In Hong Kong, most credit and debit cards do not use PIN codes, and you simply swipe the card. In some cases, ATMs and card terminals will ask for a PIN, however, HK issued PINs are usually six digitals long instead of 4 digitals in the USA and Europe. In this case, try your PIN as normal and if it does not work you will need to add two zeros before your PIN.

Tipping

Tipping is generally expected, although not compulsory, in restaurants, hotels and taxis.

Anything less than HK$10-20 would be insulting to a hotel porter who has carried your bag up to your room, but HK$10 is acceptable to the doorman who holds the taxi door open for you. You should also leave something for the maid who has serviced your room and for a stay of 5 or 6 nights, HK$100 is appropriate if you have been well looked after.

Many (but not all) restaurants automatically add a 10% service charge to your bill, but it is by no means certain that the money goes to the waiting staff. If you have been well served you should consider a 5-10 per cent addition to this.

On short taxi rides, it is appropriate to round up the fare to the nearest dollar. Give a 5-dollar tip for a longer ride.

Food Safety and Water

Hong Kong's food has an excellent reputation and is usually cooked with fresh ingredients.

Even the roadside *dai pai dongs* have a high standard of hygiene and you should have no gastric problems. If your stomach is more sensitive than most, you might want to avoid oysters and other shellfish.

Some cuts of meat that might be discarded elsewhere are readily available here, as nothing is wasted. If you like to try new food, there are plenty of opportunities!

Some of the cheaper restaurants use MSG in their ingredients and you should ask if you are sensitive to this. Peanut oil may also be used and those with peanut

allergies should check before ordering.

Unless the plumbing in your building is very old, it is safe to drink tap water. Your hotel will probably provide you with bottled water, however, and it can be cheaply bought at all convenience stores and supermarkets. Hong Kong Disneyland on-site hotels provide several large bottles of water to guests every day, but the tap water is safe to drink both in the hotels and in the theme park.

Languages: The Cantonese Dialect

The locally spoken Chinese dialect is Cantonese. This is also spoken in the major Southern Chinese city of Guangzhou just 70 miles to the north, and in other parts of neighbouring Guangdong province. The national language of China is Mandarin which is very different.

Chinese people from different linguistic areas may not understand each other's speech but the written form of the language (either using traditional or simplified characters) is universally understood.

There has been a recent influx of Mainland Chinese settling in Hong Kong and tourism from the Mainland has boomed since the dramatic expansion of the Chinese economy, so you are very likely to hear Mandarin spoken.

It is also the preferred second language in the numerous international English medium schools and it is the language spoken by the greatest number of people in the world.
Public announcements are made in Cantonese, English and Mandarin and many local people can converse in all three.

Cantonese is not an easy language to learn for the Westerner. Although most Cantonese words are single syllable, the dialect uses eight distinct tones, which are often quite hard to distinguish to the untrained ear. Many expatriates learn some survival phrases and a few are listed here, using 'pinyin' phonetics.
jo-sahn – good morning
neh ho mah ? – how are you?
gai do cheen ah? – how much is it?
d'jun jaw – turn left
d'jun yau – turn right
yee doh – stop here
m'goy – thank you

There are many Cantonese phrasebooks available if you have a good ear for languages and would like to learn more. Locals will be impressed.

Is English widely spoken?
Conveniently, a significant number of Hongkongers can speak English to some degree - although in parts of the New Territories this is not always the case. In hotels, shops and restaurants English is widely spoken and understood, as well as throughout Hong Kong Disneyland where everyone speaks English well. You may have more trouble with taxi-drivers though, so Uber may be a good option for transport.

The British influence is still very much in evidence in street signs and place names and it is quite rare to find written signs or public information that are not in Chinese characters accompanied by an English translation.

Mobile Phones, Internet Access and Wi-Fi

Roaming
Your first option to use your phone in Hong Kong is to use roaming on the SIM card that you use at home, if it is enabled. However, the cost of this is often exorbitant – check with your provider for pricing; some offer this service for a low daily or monthly fee or no fee at all, others charge hugely expensive rates.

This is the simplest option as there is nothing to do (except enabling roaming on your phone). You keep your phone number and don't need to swap out any SIM cards – it just works.

SIM Card
Buying a local sim card can be complicated, so it is better to get one designed for foreign travellers and pick it up at the airport. This SIM card will allow you to use data while in Hong Kong. Pricing is very affordable – approx. £6/US$7/€7/HK$55 for unlimited data for 8 days. There are many other services available.

We recommend looking at Klook and comparing which option works best for you. This website is an excellent one-stop-shop for entertainment and tickets in Asia. The above SIM card can be purchased at bit.ly/hksim.

You can get an exclusive HK$40 discount on your first booking by signing up at this special link - bit.ly/klookinvite.

E-SIM
If you are a modern smartphone that supports the feature, then we highly recommend an E-SIM instead. This is a virtual sim card that is added to your phone. You still keep your normal sim card and phone number to receive phone calls and texts but can use data using a virtual sim card. It is as simple as paying for your E-sim and then scanning a QR code on your phone to activate it – there is no need to order a card and then physically pick it up upon arrival. We recommend looking at Airalo – www.bit.ly/gotoairalo – plans will vary with current offers including 1GB for US$3.5, 3GB for US$7 and 5GB for US$10.50 with operator HKMobile. Alternatively, Hong Kong Unicom offers 8 days of unlimited data for US$9.

As of April 2020, the

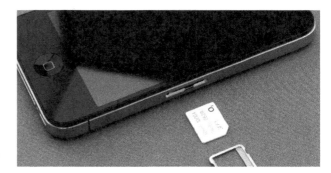

compatible devices are iPhone XR and later, Samsung Galaxy S20/S20+/S20 Ultra/Z Flip/Fold, Nuu Mobile X5, Google Pixel 3/3XL/4/4XL/3a/3a XL, Lenovo Yoga 630, HP Spectre Folio, iPad Air and Pro (3rd Gen), iPad Mini (5th Gen), Gemini PDA, and Motorola Razr 2019.

Wi-Fi Rental
There are also Wi-Fi hotspot rental services such as Uroaming which are present at the airports. You

can also book this on Klook at bit.ly/hkwifiroam from HK$18 per day per device.

Unlike in mainland China, internet access in Hong Kong is not censored by the local government.

There is free Wi-Fi throughout the Disneyland hotels. At the theme park, Wi-Fi is only available near the park entrance, in most shopping and dining areas and along the parade route.

Climate

Hong Kong has a sub-tropical climate with seasonal variations. It has cool winters and hot, humid summers. Winter temperatures can fall to as low as 8°C Celsius (46°F).

It is warm, sunny and dry in the autumn and hot, humid and rainy from spring to summer.

The summer months from May until September get uncomfortably hot with temperatures up to 34°C (93°F) and high percentages of humidity. The wettest month is May and the driest is January. The average annual rainfall is 2638.3 mm

(103.9 inches).

Hong Kong is a busy tourist destination throughout the year but the most pleasant weather is often in October and November. This is when the humidity drops and the days often become warm and sunny. The least comfortable months are July and August, although even September is often uncomfortably humid.

Hong Kong suffers from severe rainstorms as well as occasional typhoons. The government has installed sophisticated warning systems for heavy rain and typhoons. Numbered warning signals are issued by

the Hong Kong Observatory and hoisted in government buildings, together with appropriate recommendations depending on the proximity of the centre or eye of the typhoon. The word 'typhoon' is from the Cantonese *tai fung* – meaning big wind.

Local newspapers, television and radio stations also keep people informed of progress if a typhoon is in the area, and the Observatory publishes frequent weather updates (www.hko.gov.hk). Hong Kong Disneyland is well prepared for all these eventualities.

Getting There

Getting to Hong Kong Disneyland is easy – Hong Kong is extremely well connected by its international airport to most of the world and can be accessed by other means too.

From Hong Kong International Airport

The majority of visitors arrive by plane at Hong Kong International Airport *(Chek Lap Kok)* on Lantau Island (the same island as Disneyland). More than 68 million passengers passed through the airport in 2015 and it is not an exaggeration to say that it runs like clockwork.

There are direct flights to Hong Kong from major cities in Asia, Europe, Africa, North America and Oceania and by transfer from almost everywhere else. All of the world's major airlines have connections with Hong Kong.

The local Hong Kong-owned flagship carrier is Cathay Pacific and it operates more than 140 planes flying worldwide. Several budget airlines are also headquartered here, including Hong Kong Airlines, Hong Kong Express and Air Hong Kong.

Hong Kong International Airport handles 1,100 daily flights. More than half of the World's population live within a five-hour flight from Hong Kong, and over 73,000 people work at the airport.

The shortest approximate flight times (in hours) from some major cities are: New York 16.5, Toronto 16, Cape Town 15.5, London 12.5, Auckland 12, Cairo 10.5, Moscow 9.5, Sydney 9 and Dubai 8.

Via MTR

The transport links to and from the airport run efficiently. Follow the clear signs at the arrival halls for the Airport Express. This railway is operated by the Hong Kong Mass Transit Railway (MTR). You can get to downtown Hong Kong in just over 20 minutes. However, to get to Disneyland, requires some backtracking and two train changes.

First, take the Airport Express toward Hong Kong and exit at Tsing Yi Station. Here change to the Tung Chung line towards Tung Chung and exit at Sunny Bay station. At Sunny Bay station take the cute Disneyland Resort Line to Disneyland Resort. In total, this will take about 45 minutes with perfect connections or closer to 1 hour realistically.

By Disneyland Resort Station, you can either catch a free shuttle bus to the three Disney hotels (allow another 15 to 20 minutes with waiting time), or you can leave your luggage in storage (HK$130 per item) and head straight to the theme park or have it transferred to a Disney hotel for the same charge.

The cost of the journey is HK$65 with an Octopus transit card (buy this at the airport station) or HK$86.50 with a Single Journey ticket.

Via Taxi or Uber

If you are catching a taxi, follow the sign and a helpful airport employee stationed there will ask for your destination and direct you to the correct queue. The Uber pickup point is different so follow the instructions in the app.

These options are the most practical for most travellers as the airport is only a 15-minute drive from the airport and you can be dropped off directly at your hotel if staying on-site. Taxis are metered and the price is usually HK$100-$140 (~£10-£14 or US$13-$18).

This means that for 2 people, the price is the same for a taxi as public transport, and even for one person, it is only a small premium for a big time-saving.

Uber prices are very similar, although possibly marginally cheaper, and offer the convenience of in-app payment.

Many hotels in Hong Kong will arrange an airport transfer directly to your hotel and you will be met after Customs.

Whichever way you leave the airport it is likely to be quick and efficient. We recommend a taxi or Uber.

From Downtown Hong Kong

A new addition to Hong Kong Disneyland's services is the Hong Kong Disneyland Magic Gateway. This is located in downtown Hong Kong at Hong Kong West Kowloon Station (Near Arrival Concourse, Exit A).

Here, you can check in to your Hong Kong Disneyland Hotel and check-in your luggage which will be transferred to your Disney hotel allowing you a more hassle-free journey without luggage. You can also purchase theme park tickets here. This is a great option if you are visiting downtown Hong Kong before Disneyland.

Finally, there is also a free shuttle bus service from here to Hong Kong Disneyland, although this is marketed as being for guests who arrive via the High-Speed Cross-Border Train into the station from China. You can ask to see if they will make any exceptions.

Via MTR
If you are coming from Kowloon, take the Tung Chung Line to Sunny Bay and then the Disneyland Resort Line. The travel time is about 35 minutes and the

fare is HK$20.70 with an octopus card or HK$24.50 with a single ticket. From East Tsim Tsa Tsui the fare is the same with a journey time of around 50 minutes. From Central Station on Hong Kong Island to Disneyland the journey time is 40 minutes and costs HK$26.10 with Octopus and $30 with a Single Fare ticket.

Just by Disneyland Resort Station, you can either catch a shuttle bus to the three Disney hotels (allow another 15 to 20 minutes with waiting time), or you can leave your luggage in storage (HK$130 per item) and head straight to the theme park or have it transferred to a Disney hotel for the same charge.

You can use an app such as Google Maps or Citymapper to find the quickest MTR journey from your location.

Via Taxi or Uber
From Kowloon or TST to Disneyland will take about 25 minutes by taxi and cost around HK$210 to HK$250. From the Central Station area is a journey of about 30 minutes with a fare of HK$230 to HK$290. Uber prices are comparable to a taxi.

In this case, the taxi costs around ten times the price of the MTR and is usually about twice as fast. If going to one of the Disney hotels, the taxi can drop you off right at the hotel itself or at the theme park.

Via Ferry
Finally, you have the option of a ferry from Hong Kong to Disneyland. This is slower than the MTR, more expensive and arrives well after the park opens and leaves well before closing time at a pier about a 5-minute walk from the park (and about 5 minutes from Hong Kong Disneyland Hotel). It is probably much less crowded and more relaxing than the MTR, but we cannot recommend it for a full day in the parks due to the timing. See the Star Ferry website for current timings at starferry.com.hk. Pricing is HK$160 for a roundtrip.

Hotels

Hong Kong Disneyland is still very much in its infancy, and when building the resort, it was estimated that most guests would only visit the theme park for one day. Therefore, there are only three on-site hotels available – *Disney's Hollywood Hotel, Disney Explorers Lodge* and *Hong Kong Disneyland Hotel*.

In all honestly, the price difference between the three hotels is minimal – in low season, for example, a Standard Room costs the same at all three hotels (HK$1,980). During peak season, the three categories of hotel become clearer with the *Hollywood Hotel* being the most affordable and the *Hong Kong Disneyland Hotel* being the most expensive, with *Disney Explorers Lodge* in the middle. As such, it is the different amenities and room options that will help you make your choice.

As well as the proximity to the theme park, the main benefits of booking a Disney hotel are:

• At least one Attraction Priority Admission Pass for at attraction of your choice
• Complimentary Vouchers valued at up to HK$480 to be used on hotel table service restaurants, dinner buffets, Quick Service restaurants in the park, popcorn buckets, hotel stores and at the *Bibbidi Bobbidi Boutique*.
• In-hotel character experiences
• Complimentary Transportation & Parking
• Luggage storage services
• Friendly and knowledgeable Disney Cast Members at the hotel
• Dedicated security and park entrance lanes

Unlike all other Disney theme parks, there is no early theme park entry at Hong Kong Disneyland for Disney hotel guests.

Other Hotels

Due to its rural isolated location, there are no hotels near Hong Kong Disneyland which are not run by Disney. Your best option if not wanting to stay at a Disney hotel would be to stay in downtown Hong Kong where there is a huge choice for all budgets and tastes, or by the airport (Tung Chung area) for a more limited selection.

We recommend booking these other hotels either directly on their website or through an aggregator such as www.hotels.com or www.expedia.com

Hong Kong Disneyland Hotel

The 400-room Hong Kong Disneyland Hotel is the most luxurious of the Disney resorts. The resort is themed to the Victorian period with the interior resembling a palace of this era. This hotel has the widest range of amenities of the three on-site hotels and the best dining selection.

The Hong Disneyland Hotel is the closest hotel to the theme park being just 850m (a 10-minute walk) from the entrance. A complimentary shuttle service is also available, although this is slower than walking. The shuttle bus ride is about 5 to 10 minutes, plus a 5-minute walk from the bus stop to the theme park entrance.

The hotel features an outdoor pool with a water slide, an indoor pool, a sauna, a steam room and a hot tub, as well as a gym with a decent range of equipment. There is also a tennis court, a multi-court for football, a children's playground, and a classic English-style garden maze.

You can add extra thematic touches to rooms by adding decoration packages for HK$500-1100 – these include slippers, towels, amenity kits and other theming and can be chosen to celebrate occasions such as birthdays, weddings or anniversaries. You can also add character-themed decorations with Duffy, Toy Story and Moana as options.

You will also find live music in the lobby from a jazz band or pianist, a complimentary children's activity centre called 'Storybook Playroom', tai chi in the morning with Master Goofy, Disney character meets by the grand staircase, and "Disney's Story Time" in the evening where Cast Members retell Disney tales as they walk through a giant storybook.

There is a concierge-level of the hotel on the top floor called Kingdom Club. Kingdom Club guests have access to a lounge with light food and drink throughout the day, as well as a complimentary first-round minibar and exclusive kids' activities such as crafts making, a bedtime story and a Disney character in their pyjamas at bedtime. As well as regular rooms and suites, there are also special Cinderella-themed and Frozen-themed suites are also available.

The hotel also has a *Bibbidi Bobbidi Boutique* makeover salon where little girls can be transformed into princesses with make-up, hair styling and an (optional) princess dress, as well as photos as a souvenir. Reservations can be made by calling +852 3510-6000 or at the gift shop at the Hong Kong Disneyland Hotel. The experience lasts 30 minutes to 1 hour depending on the package chosen – pricing is from HK$980 to HK$2,180. This is open to non-hotel guests too.

The hotel does not have any Quick Service dining locations, except the outdoor pool-side Sea Breeze Bar.

Guests who book a standard room or deluxe room receive one Attraction Priority Admission Pass. Guests who stay in a Sea View Room receive three of these passes, as well as seat reservations to *Festival of the Lion King*. Guests staying in a Kingdom Club receive seat reservations to *Mickey and the Wondrous Book* and four Priority Admission Passes.

Breakfast: Not included.

Room Prices: (all prices include a 10% service charge not displayed when initially booking through the Disney website – regular discounts are available on these prices)

• Standard Room – HK$1,980 to HK$4,235
• Deluxe Room – HK$2,090 to HK$4,455
• Sea View Room – HK$2,310 to HK$4,675
• Kingdom Club Room – HK$5,510 to HK$7,040
• Kingdom Club Suite – HK$7,150 to HK$9,790
• Kingdom Club Frozen or Cinderella Suite – HK$9,130 to HK$11,990
• Walt Disney Suite (196 m², sleeps up to 6 people) – HK$33,000

Extras: Complimentary Wi-Fi, ATM, babysitting services, business centre services, currency exchange, dry cleaning and laundry service, shuttle service to downtown Hong Kong, mail service, package shipping, and package express.

Dining

Crystal Lotus – Table Service. Chinese cuisine. Serves dim sum, barbecued meat, soup, noodles, rice, abalone, and other meat and seafood dishes. Lunch 8-dish meals are HK$318-378 (minimum 4 guests). A la carte options are also available. Dim is available at lunch only. On weekends and public holidays, there is also signature Disney character-shaped dim sum available for HK$88-108 per 2 to 4 dim sum pieces (you need to order this at least 24 hours in advance).

Enchanted Garden Restaurant – Buffet with Disney characters. This is very popular and reservations are recommended, especially for breakfast. Pricing is HK$348 per adult and HK$228 per child for breakfast, HK$398-438 per adult and HK$258-288 at lunch, and HK$618-788 per adult and $HK408-528 per child for dinner. Lunch and dinner prices depend on the chosen seating time.

Walt's Café – Table Service. Breakfast items include an American breakfast set, a Chinese breakfast set and eggs benedict. Breakfast prices are HK$115 for children or HK$178-198 for adults. Set lunches are HK$328 per adult and HK$228 per child. The afternoon tea menu is HK$458 for 2 people and includes scones, mini pastries, mini desserts and tea. With the Garden and Grilled menu, you order a main course (such as lobster or steak) and receive access to a salad bar as well as lobster bisque and a drink for HK$488-568. Desserts are $98-138 each. Kids meals are HK$115-308. This is our favourite restaurant at Hong Kong Disneyland and we feel the 'Garden and Grilled' menu is excellent value for a great meal.

Sea Breeze Bar – Pool-side bar with snacks. Open seasonally. Serves snacks such as barbecue skewers, chicken wings, fish and chips, pizza, and chicken croissants priced at HK$128-168. Also serves ice creams, chips and prawn crackers (HK$22-42). Serves cocktails and sangria (HK$80), mocktails (HK$68), and beer, soft drinks & wine (HK$48-58).

Disney Explorers Lodge

This 750-room deluxe hotel is the newest hotel at Hong Kong Disneyland. It is themed around the idea of exploration and adventure. The resort has rooms and areas themed to the four tropical areas of Asia, Africa, Oceania and South America.

This is our recommended Disney hotel to stay at – it is fun, in a great location and is the most unique. The hotel features large, modern rooms. This hotel is more expensive than *Disney's Hollywood Hotel* but less expensive than the *Hong Kong Disneyland Hotel*.

The Explorers Lodge features beautiful gardens, and a large outdoor pool. There is no on-site gym, but you can walk to the *HK Disneyland Hotel* in 5 to 10 minutes and use the facilities there.

This hotel hosts an afternoon poolside party at the Rain Drop Pool with games and activities.

Guests can learn about plants and cultures in four themed gardens. They can even collect four special stamps for each region. The hotel features over 700 varieties of plants.

Kids also have access to an indoor play area called Nemo's Underwater Reef.

To reach the theme park there is the option of walking or the complimentary shuttle bus. The walk is about 20 minutes (although it is mostly shaded, this is uncomfortable in summer humidity). The shuttle bus ride is about 5 to 10 minutes, plus a 5-minute walk from the bus stop to the theme park entrance.

Guests in a standard room or deluxe room receive one Attraction Priority Admission Pass. Guests in a Sea View Room receive three passes, and

reservations to *Festival of the Lion King*.

Breakfast: Not included.

Room Prices:
• Standard Room – HK$1,980 to HK$3,025
• Deluxe Room – HK$2,090 to HK$3,190
• Sea View Room – HK$2,200 to HK$3,575

Extras: Complimentary Wi-Fi, ATM, babysitting services, currency exchange, dry cleaning and laundry service, shuttle service to downtown Hong Kong, mail service, package shipping, and package express.

Dining

Dragon Wind – Table Service. Chinese and International Cuisine. Serves soups, seafood, casseroles, pork, beef, poultry, tofu, dim sum and veggie dishes. A 7-dish set menu is HK$478, and sharing platters for 4 guests are HK$1580-1780. A la carte dining is available.

World of Color – Table Service. World cuisine. Serves salads, pork chop, salmon, pasta, pizza, noodles, pad thai, steaks and much more. Set menus range from HK$888-$1328 for 2 people. A la carte mains are HK$168-348. Kids meals are HK$158.

Chart Room Café – Quick Service. For breakfast: serves puff pastries, Mickey waffles, congee, pastries, and stir-fried noodles. The rest of the day you will find flatbread, pork chop, mac and cheese, beef short rib, and fish and chicken wing platters. Also serves gelato. Breakfast set menus are HK$120-130. All-day set menus are HK$135-155.

Dreamer's Lookout – Snacks, drinks and luxury chocolate shop. HK$25-80 each.

Disney's Hollywood Hotel

Disney's Hollywood Hotel is the most affordable of the three on-site hotels. This 600-room hotel has a fun art-Deco Hollywood theme.

To reach the theme park, there is the option of walking or the complimentary shuttle bus. The walk is about 20 minutes (although this is mostly shaded, this is uncomfortable in summer humidity).

The shuttle bus ride is about 5 to 10 minutes, plus a 5-minute walk from the bus stop to the theme park entrance. This hotel is marginally further away than Disney Explorers Lodge.

The hotel features an outdoor Piano-shaped pool, a courtyard with photo opportunities including a vintage car, an outside playground and a games arcade. The resort does not have a gym, but hotel guests may use the gym at the Hong Kong Disneyland Hotel at no charge.

Daily activities include "Morning Movie Time with Goofy" where you can watch Disney classics and meet Goofy, arts and crafts sessions, outdoor games

with Cast Members including vehicle rides, and Disney movie showings in the evening by the pool. You can also see characters in the hotel lobby at certain times of the day.

Guests who book a standard room or deluxe room receive one Attraction Priority Admission Pass. Guests who stay in a Sea View Room receive three passes.

The price difference between this hotel and Disney Explorers Lodge is minimal.

Breakfast: Not included.

Room Prices:
• Standard Room – HK$1,980 to HK$2,915
• Deluxe Room – HK$2,090 to HK$3,080
• Sea View Room – HK$2,200 to HK$3,520
• Hollywood Suite with separate living room– HK$4,620

Extras: Complimentary Wi-Fi, ATM, babysitting services, business centre services, currency exchange, dry cleaning and laundry service, shuttle service to downtown Hong Kong, mail service, package shipping, and package express.

Dining

Chef Mickey – Buffet restaurant and meet Chef Mickey. Buffet available for breakfast (HK$258 per adult, HK$168 per child) as well as lunch (HK$338-388 per adult, HK$218-248 per child) and dinner (HK$548 per adult, HK$358 per child). An a la carte menu is served instead of the buffet Monday to Friday at lunchtime, and Monday to Thursday at dinnertime with individual entrees costing HK$148-198.

Hollywood & Dine – Quick Service. Serves pork chop, curry chicken, beef patty with rice, braised beef, dim sum platter and vegetable pasta. Entrees are HK$72 to HK$148.

Studio Lounge – Food and drinks lounge. Serves salad, fish and chips, barbecue skewers, cheeseburger, spaghetti Bolognese, pizza, nasi goreng, stir-fried beef, Indian meals and vegetarian meals. Entrees cost HK$138-208. Kids meals are HK$115. Also serves cocktails and sangria (HK$80), mocktails (HK$68), and beer, soft drinks & wine (HK$48-58).

Tickets

There are many ways to buy park entry tickets for Hong Kong Disneyland. Prices, special offers and ticket lengths vary depending on where you buy your tickets. To help you choose the best option for you, here is a detailed look at your ticket options.

Guests should purchase tickets in advance online to take advantage of any special offers. Compared to the Western Disney theme parks, tickets here are relatively cheap. You can purchase a theme park ticket for 1 or 2 days.

Unlike at most other Disney theme parks, Hong Kong Disneyland does not vary the standard price of its tickets according to visitor expectations, so tickets are the same price year-round.

The Official Website
The first option is to buy tickets on the official website hongkongdisneyland.com.

At the time of writing, the standard prices are as follows:
● 1 Day Ticket – HK$639 per adult, HK$475 per child, HK$100 per senior
● 1 Day Ticket with 1 meal plus 1 snack – HK$755 per adult, HK$600 per child
● 2 Day Ticket – HK$825 per adult, HK$609 per child, HK$170 per senior

However, there are also special offers which mean you shouldn't pay these prices. These vary from time to time but at the time of writing include:
● 1 Day "Play, Shop, Eat" Ticket – this is the same price as the standard 1-day

ticket but also includes a snack voucher and HK$10 merchandise voucher.
● 2 Day "Fun" Ticket – HK$719 per adult and HK$535 per child for 2 visits within a 7-day period. Also include two HK$10 merchandise vouchers and a buy-one-get-one-free Popcorn voucher.
● 2 Day "Double the Happiness" Offer – HK$739 per adult and HK$549 per child for 2 visits within a designated period. Plus, 1 Meal Combo at one of the designated restaurants (valued up to HK$130). This is the best deal of all and is cheaper than buying even a one-day ticket plus a meal, and you get a second day in the park too.

Top Tip: If you buy from the official website, sign up for a free MyDisneyFans account on the Hong Kong Disneyland website and then sign-in before buying your tickets. You will get extra benefits such as: free luggage tags, a HK$20 merchandise discount coupon, 50% discount on a combo meals after the first full-price combo meal, free popcorn when buying a popcorn bucket, 15% discount on the afternoon tea set at Main Street Corner Café and more.

Tickets from Klook.com
You can also buy tickets on other reseller websites such

as Klook - bit.ly/hkdistickets (this ticket also includes a meal in the park). You can get an exclusive discount on your first Klook booking by signing up at this special link - bit.ly/klookref. On top of this, Klook regularly sells standard admission tickets for a lower price than direct through Disney. At the time of writing, for example, a one-day ticket is HK$580 on Klook and HK$639 via the Disney website, and the 2-day ticket with combo meal is HK$20 cheaper per person.

Whether you buy your ticket via the Disneyland website or Klook, you will have a QR code which you scan to get into the park – you can scan on a phone or print it out.

At a Disney Hotel
If you are staying at a Disney hotel, then you can buy the tickets at the hotel itself when you arrive, paying with either cash or card.

Annual Passes

Another option you may wish to consider is getting an Annual Pass to the park as it works out to be a good deal for extended visits. It is also a good way to save money if you visit two or more times within a year (e.g. visiting in August 2020 and then July 2021).

Hong Kong Disneyland calls its annual pass Magic Access.

There are three main types of pass – Silver, Gold and Platinum.

Silver Pass

HK$1,279 per adult, HK$915 per child or full-time student (ages 12-25) and HK$316 per senior

Silver Pass benefits:
• 220 days of park access on weekdays, no access during some peak periods
• 10% off dining in the park and hotels, except certain locations
• 10% off merchandise
• 10% off hotels, except certain dates
• Discounted parking
• On your birthday, buy 2 get 1 free on hotel dinner buffets on weekdays

Gold Pass

HK$2,059 per adult, HK$1,459 per child or full-time student and HK$525 per senior

Gold Pass benefits:
• 340 days of park access, no access during some peak periods
• 10% off dining in the park and hotels, except certain locations
• 10% off merchandise
• 15% off hotels, except certain dates
• Free parking 24 times per year. Discounted parking after that.
• One additional Fastpass per visit
• On your birthday, buy 2 get 1 free on hotel dinner buffets
• 50% discount on stroller rentals (except 24 to 31 December)

Platinum Pass

HK$3,599 per adult, HK$2,569 per child or full-time student and HK$890 per senior

Platinum Pass benefits:
• 365 days of park access
• 25% off dining in the park and hotels, except certain locations
• 20% off merchandise
• 20% off hotels, except certain dates
• Free parking in a designated area
• One additional Fastpass per visit
• Online seat reservation for *Mickey and the Wondrous Book*
• 10% discount on 1-day tickets (up to 6 per year)
• On your birthday, buy 1 get 1 free on hotel dinner buffets
• Much more

You can check the blockout dates (dates you cannot enter the park) for the Silver and Gold pass one year in advance at hongkongdisneyland.com/magic-access/blockout-dates/.

Top Tip: It may make sense to buy the Silver Pass for one person in your party for the hotel, shopping and dining discounts.

A Note on Tickets

Children are classified as being aged between 3 and 11 years old. Children below age 3 receive free park admission. Seniors are classed as those aged 65 and above.

Eligible guests with disabilities can enjoy a 30% discount on one-day tickets. The ticket must be purchased at the Park's ticket booth. An original copy of a valid Registration Card for People with Disabilities issued by the Labour and Welfare Bureau of the Government of Hong Kong must be presented upon ticket purchase. Seniors do not get an additional discount for being disabled – they purchase a standard senior ticket.

Understanding the Park

Before taking a detailed look at the theme park, we think it is best to explain some of the services on offer at Hong Kong Disneyland, including Fastpass, the Hong Kong Disneyland app, and more.

When to Visit

Crowds at Hong Kong Disneyland vary significantly from season to season and even day to day. The difference in a single day can save you hours in queue lines over the day. You need to consider national and school holidays in Hong Kong, Mainland China and surrounding countries, as well as the weather and pricing, to find the best time to go.

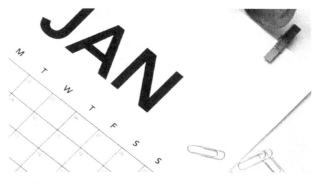

Here is our guide of the best times to visit Hong Kong Disneyland, even including a detailed analysis of weekdays.

Major Holidays In 2020 (Times to Avoid)
• 1st to 5th January: New Year's Day & School Break
• 24th January to 1st February: Chinese New Year and HK School Holidays
• 28th March to 5th April: School Holidays in Mainland China
• 10th April to 19th April: Easter and School Holidays in Hong Kong
• 30th April to 3rd May: Buddha's Birthday and Labor Day Weekend
• Mid-June to mid-August: Summer School Holidays
• 25th September to 7th October: Mid-Autumn Festival and Golden Week

• 24th to 26th October: Double Ninth Festival Weekend
• 12th December 2020 to 4th January 2021 – Winter School Holidays

Ideal times to visit are therefore: most of January to March, May, early June, late August to mid-September, most of mid-October to mid-December. Watch out for any holidays during these times, though.

Days of the Week
The days of the week that you visit make a tremendous difference to how long you will wait to get on rides. A ride can have a wait time of 60 minutes on one day, and just 5 minutes the next. The most notable difference is between weekends and

weekdays, so try to avoid weekends if possible.

The best days of the week to visit are Tuesday, Wednesday and Thursday, then Friday and Monday. Saturday and Sunday are busier than weekdays year-round. Park hours are often longer on weekends to compensate for the larger crowds; despite this, Hong Kong Disneyland is still much less busy than the other Disney parks.

Specific Dates
As well as the above information to guide your visit, you can use the Hong Kong Disneyland website to simulate booking a hotel room. The higher the price, the higher the expected attendance for that date.

Hong Kong Disneyland App

Hong Kong Disneyland has a free Apple iOS and Android app, which allows you to enhance your trip.

You can check the opening hours, timings of shows and parades, and even see the attraction wait times. You can also see whether restaurants are open or closed, and individual lands – this is particularly important as, during quieter periods, entire lands in the park alternate closing early and certain restaurants may not open.

You will need a data connection to see live information, which means you must connect to the in-park Wi-Fi or use a data connection. We would recommend a data connection as the in-park Wi-Fi is only available near the park entrance, in most shopping and dining areas and along the parade route.

The app is translated into English for your convenience.

On-Ride Photos

Some of Hong Kong Disneyland's rides have cameras positioned and timed to take perfect on-ride photos of you at the most action-filled moments on attractions. Buy the picture and see yourself at the fastest, steepest, scariest, and most fun moment of the ride. These make for timeless keepsakes.

When you get off selected rides, you will walk past screens that preview your photo (with a watermark on top). If you wish to purchase it, go to the photo counter.

You do not have to buy on-ride photos straight after your ride; you can pick them up at any time that same day. Just remember your unique number at the ride exit or ask a member of staff at the photo kiosk to write it down for you.

If you like the photo, Cast Members will show it to you up close before you pay for it. If you like it, buy it! You will treasure the photo for a long time.

The attractions with on-ride photos are *Space Mountain* and *The Many Adventures of Winnie the Pooh*.

You can get on-ride photos included with other park photos as part of Photopass (see page 25).

Package Express

The Package Express service allows you to buy an item at any of the theme park shops and pick it up later.

When paying for your goods, ask to use the Package Express Service. You will leave the item with the Cast Member who served you. When you have finished your day at the park, you pick up your item.

You can either pick up your purchases next to Guest Services after the turnstiles (to the right after the turnstiles) outside the park from 12:00pm, or at the bell service desks at the Disney hotels.

This means that you can collect all your items in one spot, even if you have multiple items from different shops.

The Package Express service is only available until about three hours before the park closes.

This service allows you to be free to eat, shop, ride attractions and watch shows to your heart's content without carrying any bags.

Fastpass

Hong Kong Disneyland offers a unique skip-the-queue system called Fastpass at no cost. It allows you to reserve a time slot for certain attractions, return at an appointed time, and ride with little to no wait. While waiting for your Fastpass reservation time, you can do something else such as shop, dine, watch a show, or experience another attraction.

How to use Fastpass

1. Choose your Fastpass ride
Two attractions at Hong Kong Disneyland offer Fastpass – Hyperspace Mountain in Tomorrowland and The Many Adventures of Winnie the Pooh in Fantasyland. It is important to recognise that only these two rides use the Fastpass system.

2. Check the wait time using the app and decide
At a Fastpass-enabled attraction, there are two ride entrances – the standby entrance where you can queue up and ride (e.g. 45-minute wait), and the Fastpass entrance.

If the standby wait time is short, use the regular standby entrance. If the wait is too long for you, then you should use the Fastpass system. If the standby wait is less than 20 minutes, we recommend waiting in the standby queue. This is because Fastpasses often require you to backtrack across the park negating

time savings.

3. Get your Fastpass
Near the ride entrance is the Fastpass distribution area with machines and a screen showing the current return time for Fastpass reservations (e.g. 14:15 to 15:15). This is the time your reservation is made for and is printed on Fastpasses.

Go to the Fastpass machines and scan your park ticket or annual pass. The machine will print a paper Fastpass telling you the time of your reservation. This is the same as that shown on the screen above the entrance. Keep your Fastpass and park ticket safe.

4. Wait
Dine, explore the park, or enjoy another ride or show until your Fastpass return time.

5. Return and Ride
Return to the ride during the time window on your Fastpass, entering through

the ride's Fastpass entrance. Hand your Fastpass to the Cast Member at the Fastpass entrance who will keep it.

Now, you can ride within a few minutes, skipping the regular queue – the wait time with a Fastpass is often under 5 minutes but can be up to 15 minutes.

The Fastpass System Explained

Now that you have read about the advantages of the Fastpass system, we have to tell you the system's limitations - namely that you cannot use Fastpasses to avoid waiting at every single attraction.

Firstly, not every ride offers Fastpass - only two rides in the park offer this service. Secondly, you can only hold one Fastpass ticket at a time, though there are exceptions to this as noted below.

Therefore, you will likely use Fastpass once or twice throughout your time at Hong Kong Disneyland.

How Fastpass works:
Every Hong Kong Disneyland entry ticket and annual pass includes Fastpass access – it is a free system which is available to every guest.

Each day, Disney will decide

what percentage of riders they want to be able to use the Fastpass system. Let's say that in this case, it is 50%.

So, assuming 2000 guests per hour can ride *Space Mountain*, the Fastpass system will distribute 1000 Fastpass tickets for each operating hour. This means 50% of guests will use Fastpass to board, and 50% will use the standby queue each hour.

There are, therefore, a limited number of Fastpass tickets for each ride each hour. This is to ensure that the standby queue line is kept to a reasonable level.

The first Fastpass return time for an attraction is usually 30 minutes after park opening, although sometimes it is later.

Fastpass slots then move in

5-minute increments so after all the Fastpasses for 10:30am-11:30am are distributed, the next return time will be 10:35am-11:35am. Once all Fastpasses have been distributed for the day, the ticket distribution machines are shut down.

Rides may not offer Fastpasses for the entire park operating hours for operational reasons.

If you want to know the time of the last Fastpass return, ask the Cast Members at the attraction. When Fastpass stops being used, the regular queue usually moves twice as quickly.

Is Fastpass always available?
Yes. Even during times of very low attendance, the Fastpass system is operational.

Get Extra Fastpasses

Officially you can only hold one Fastpass at a time. However, there are exceptions.

• When your Fastpass return time begins, you can get another Fastpass even if you have not used your current Fastpass yet. E.g. You have a *Space Mountain* Fastpass for 14:00-15:00. You can get another

Fastpass from 14:00.

• Cast Members (at their discretion) may allow you to use a Fastpass after the return time, though not before. We recommend you stick to the listed times.

• If your return time is over two hours away, you can get a second Fastpass two hours after picking up the first.

E.g. You got a *Space Mountain* Fastpass at 10:00; the return time is 15:00-16:00. As 15:00 is over two hours away from when you got your Fastpass, you can get another Fastpass at 12:00 (two hours after 10:00). You can check the time your next Fastpass is available on the bottom of your latest Fastpass ticket.

Disney "Priority Special" Attraction Admission Pass

The "Priority Special" Pass is a paid-for front-of-the-line ticket.

It is available in two versions.

Option 1 – Get priority entry to any three attractions from this list at your choice:
• *Big Grizzly Mountain Runaway Mine Cars*
• *Ant-Man and The Wasp: Nano Battle!*
• *Mystic Manor*
• *Iron Man Experience*
• *Mickey's PhilharMagic*

The cost of this option is HK$249 per person.

Option 2 – Get priority entry to all eight attractions from this list:
• All five attractions from Option 1.
• *The Many Adventures of Winnie the Pooh*
• *Toy Soldier Parachute Drop*
• *Slinky Dog Spin*

The cost of this option is HK$349 on weekdays (except public holidays), and HK$399 during weekends and public holidays.

The option can be purchased online (and combined with a park entry ticket), as well the main entrance ticket booths,

Pooh Corner and Expo Shop. Disney Hotel guests may purchase from the front desk of the three resort hotels at a discounted price.

As Hong Kong Disneyland is generally not very crowded, we do not recommend purchasing this option unless you visit on the busiest of days such as on a national holiday. Even on the busiest of days, you can see the whole park in one day. We would also recommend buying this add-on in the park so you can gauge how busy it is in reality instead of buying it before arrival.

Rider Switch

Rider Switch is a time-saving solution that allows parents to reduce queuing times when riding thrill attractions.

A common issue at theme parks is when two adults want to ride an attraction, but they have a child who is not tall enough to ride. There are three solutions:
a) the adults can take turns to ride (queuing twice);
b) one adult can choose not to experience the attraction;
c) skip the attraction.

The solution is Disney's Rider Switch, which allows

one adult to queue up and ride while the other stays with the child, then they swap without needing to queue a second time.

Each attraction implements the system in a slightly different manner so ask Cast Members at ride entrances for details.

Generally speaking, the party asks the Cast Member at the ride entrance to use Rider Switch. Enter the line with your entire party, except those not riding the first time. One or two adults will wait with the non-rider

in the Rider Switch area. The remainder of the party will experience the attraction. When the remainder of the party returns to the Rider Switch area, the guest(s) who waited with the non-rider get to ride the attraction without having to queue again.

In the case of two adults with a child, each adult will experience the ride separately, but the second adult will not need to wait to ride.

Photopass

Hong Kong Disneyland's Photopass is an easy to use system that makes collecting all your in-park photos easy.

Simply go to any in-park photographer (including those with characters) and after your photo is taken, they will give you a Photopass card so you can check your photo. You can also do this at any ride photo counter.

Next time you have a photo taken, hand over your Photopass card and the pictures will be added onto it throughout your visit and be kept together on the system. You can keep doing this anywhere you find a photographer and with on-ride photos.

You can also add an extra element of Disney magic with themed borders and details at no additional cost.

Photos are saved on the Photopass system for 30 days each from when they were taken.

Before your photos expire, visit one of the following locations to view and purchase your photos: *Town Square Photo, Space Traders, Pooh Corner, Merlin's Magic Portraits*, or the shops at the Disney hotels. At all these locations, you can purchase prints or digital versions of your Photopass photos.

Alternatively, if you just want to view or buy digital photos, download the Hong Kong Disneyland Photopass app (separate from the park app).

Pricing is HK$68 per digital photo (HK$198 for 4 digital photos), or HK$398 for all digital photos from Photopass ticket for 1 day. If you want printed photos these are HK$128 to HK$168 each for the first photo, and HK$100 to HK$130 for subsequent photos depending on the size. You

can get three printed photos for HK$268. Each printed photo also includes a digital version at no extra cost.

For those who have used Photopass or Memory Maker in the American parks or at Disneyland Paris, the Hong Kong Disneyland system works similarly.

The most significant difference, however, is the lower number of Photopass photographers throughout the Park in Hong Kong whereas there are many of them in each park in the US, allowing you to get great photos with the parks' icons.

Disney Spectacular Tour

If you want the ultimate VIP treatment, Hong Kong Disneyland is happy to oblige with its private Disney Spectacular Tour. This service is often used by celebrities, those who don't wish to wait for anything, need the extra privacy, or for guests who are very short on time.

The tour lasts for three consecutive hours and is offered for groups of up to 6 guests. Included in the price is:

• Direct entrance to rides of your choosing
• Reserved seating for live theatre shows during the tour time
• A reserved viewing area for the Disney daytime parade during the tour time
• A reserved viewing area for *Disney Paint the Night*

Pricing is HK$5,688 per party for the 3 hours; any additional hours cost HK$1,600 each. This does not include the theme park tickets, which are extra.

To learn more, or make a reservation, you can book online, email Disney at hongkongdisneyland.com/help/email/, or call the Hong Kong Disneyland Reservation Center daily between 9:00am and 8:00pm at +852 1-830-830. You can also check availability at Guest Relations on the day, but Disney recommends booking this service in advance.

Wheelchair and Stroller Rentals

Wheelchair and stroller rentals are available for guests who do not bring their own.

If your child is recently out of a stroller, it is often still worth renting one as it is likely they will get tired, due to the vast walking distances involved with a Hong Kong Disneyland visit.

Sometimes it is nice just to let kids sit in their stroller and have a break. The stroller can also be used as

an easy way to carry bags.

The daily cost of hiring a wheelchair is HK$60, or HK$30 for seniors (ages 65 and over). For a stroller, the fee is HK$140 per day. A refundable deposit of HK$100 per day is required for both stroller and wheelchair rentals.

The rental location is at the firehouse to the right of City Hall on Main Street, U.S.A. The Disney hotels also have a wheelchair rental service

that can also be used from the hotel to the park, as well as inside the park.

You are, of course, welcome to bring your own stroller or wheelchair if you wish.

When experiencing attractions, be sure to leave your stroller in the dedicated parking areas. Ask a Cast Member if you are not sure whether this is. Strollers may be moved by Cast Members to keep them neat and organised.

Lockers

There are lockers available for rental inside the theme park half-way up Main Street, U.S.A on the right. You can access the lockers as many times as you want throughout the day for a daily fee of HK$130. This is a good option to save you

carrying around items all day such as coats, backpacks and umbrellas. The locker dimensions are 45 cm x 35 cm x 43 cm (18" x 14" x 17").

If you have luggage, this cannot enter the park. A

Luggage Vallet service is available by the MTR station on Park Promenade. You can store luggage of any size here for HK$130 per item. If you are staying at a Disney hotel, they can also transfer luggage between this location and the hotel.

Spend Less Time Waiting in Queue Lines

Hong Kong Disneyland meticulously themes its queues to introduce an attraction's story before you board. However, no one likes waiting, and often you want to ride as quickly as possible. Remember that a visit to a theme park will involve waiting in queue lines; this chapter covers our top tips on minimising these waits.

1. Eat outside the regular dining hours
At Hong Kong Disneyland Resort, whether you want to eat at a Table Service restaurant or a Quick

Service meal, waiting for your food is part of the game. Have lunch before midday or after 3:00 pm for much shorter waits. Also, having dinner before 7:00 pm will reduce your time waiting. Waits of 20 minutes or longer to order are relatively typical at peak times at Quick Service restaurants.

2. Quick Service meal tricks
At Quick Service locations, each cashier has two queues, and alternates between them – count how many groups (families or friends) are in front of you

in the queue. There may be ten people in front of you in one queue line but only two families. The other queue line may have five people but from five different families. The queue with ten people will move more quickly with only two orders to process versus the other queue's five orders.

3. On-site Disney hotel guests
If you are staying at a Disney hotel you will have at least one Priority Admission Pass for an attraction. Use this to save time.

4. Get to the park before opening time

Hong Kong Disneyland allows guests into the park 30 minutes before the advertised opening time – you can then explore Main Street, U.S.A. and have something to eat, grab photos and even meet characters. If you want to meet the characters, this is the best time of the day to do so. Aim to be at the park around 45 minutes before the official opening time if you will be meeting characters so you can be one of the first in line.

5. Use FastPass and Single Rider

Earlier in this section, we covered the Fastpass system in detail. This is a free system, and you should use it to minimise waits effectively. You should be able to get both rides' Fastpasses during the day. See our chapter entitled 'Touring Plan' for more details on how to maximise your time at the park. Plus, you can also use the Single Rider queue line at *Toy Soldier Parachute Drop* to save time.

6. Skip the parades and fireworks

If you have already seen the parades, shows, or fireworks, use that time to experience rides as the wait times are often shorter during these big events – this mainly applies to the nighttime spectaculars and the daytime parade. If you have not seen the park's entertainment offerings before, we recommend you watch these. Parades and

shows are only performed at set times of the day, and most of these are as good as, if not better than, many rides.

7. Ride outdoor attractions when it rains

Outdoor attractions such as *Dumbo, Big Grizzly Mountain Runaway Mine Cars,* and *RC Racer* often have significantly reduced waits when it is raining. Yes, you may get wet while riding (a jacket will help), but the wait times will be shorter. In contrast, avoid the indoor rides when there is inclement weather as the waits will be artificially longer.

8. Choose when to visit carefully

Visit during an off-peak time if possible. If you are visiting on New Year's Day, expect to queue a lot longer than in the middle of February. Of course, weekends are busier than weekdays. See the 'When to Visit' section on page 20 to make the most of your time.

9. Shop at the end of the day

Go shopping at the end of the day on Main Street, U.S.A. Even when the park is 'officially' closed, the shops by the park entrance areas stay open longer than the rest of the park. Alternatively, go to your hotel's Disney shop, which are all open late. Shop at strategic times, and make the most of your time in the parks.

10. Get a Times Guide

Get your Park Map and the 'Today' Times Guide on the way in; you will usually find them distributed together. The 'Today' Times Guide lists all time-sensitive information at the parks such as the timings of parades, shows, character appearances, and more. As such, you will not waste time crossing the park to find out that a character you saw earlier in the day has now left a particular location. You can also check this information (plus live wait times) on the Hong Kong Disneyland app.

Doing Disney on a Budget

A visit to Hong Kong Disneyland can be pricey. However, there are ways to reduce your spending and still have a magical time.

1. Hotels – Disney hotels are themed, and offer park benefits but are also much more expensive than other hotels, such as those a few MTR stations away, or a short taxi ride away. These outside hotels can be a fraction of the price.

2. Take your own photos – If you do not want to pay for an 'official' Disney character photo, take one yourself; the Cast Members do not mind. They will even take the photo for you!

3. Take your own gifts – Buy dresses, outfits, and toys outside of Hong Kong Disneyland from Disney Stores, online, or at supermarkets before you visit the resort. Give your child the costume on arrival to avoid the high in-park merchandise prices.

4. More affordable meals – Although food prices are high, some restaurants offer better value than others – generally those selling Cantonese food instead of Western food offer the best value. Try the set menus or a buffet as a late lunch and having a lighter dinner. Also, don't buy a whole set menu – most items can be purchased individually. You can also get a park ticket which includes a meal voucher as a combo ticket and save money.

5. Park Tickets – We recommend you purchase your tickets in advance. You can either do this at the official Hong Kong Disneyland website or from other retailers. Be sure to look out for special offers.

6. Take Snacks – According to park rules, you can bring your own food and drink into the park, unlike at Tokyo Disney Resort, for example. The exact wording Disney uses is: "Guests are allowed to bring outside food and beverage items into the Park for self-consumption, provided that they do not require heating, reheating, processing, refrigeration or temperature control and do not have pungent odours. Examples of food items not permitted in the Park include, without limitation, instant noodles that require hot water, food kept in containers with reheating capabilities, and durian fruit."

There are also water fountains in the park to refill bottles – the tap water is safe to drink.

Ride Height Requirements

Certain attractions at the theme park have minimum height requirements to ride for safety reasons. These are strict and will not be bent for anyone – no matter if your child is just 0.5cm too short, these height restrictions are here for safety and are set in stone.

Here we list all of the current ride height requirements for your easy reference.

• *Toy Soldier Parachute Drop* – 81cm
• *Hyperspace Mountain* – 102cm
• *Iron Man Experience* – 102cm
• *Big Grizzly Mountain Runaway Mine Cars* – 112cm
• *RC Racer* – 120cm

Remember that just because your child may meet the height requirement doesn't mean that they won't be scared of the ride, and vice-versa.

Meeting the Characters

For many visitors, meeting characters is the highlight of their trip. Playing with Pluto, talking to Cinderella, and hugging Mickey makes for magical memories.

Note: The characters are very popular at this park and there are many opportunities to meet them. Waits for characters are often longer than waits for the rides at Hong Kong Disneyland. All characters understand English.

Hong Kong Disneyland: Certain characters are scheduled to appear around the park throughout the day. Appearance times will appear on the official park app.

On Main Street U.S.A., you can meet Mickey, Minnie, Donald and Daisy on Town Square. By Main Street Cinema, you can meet Duffy and Friends, and elsewhere on Main Street you can meet Goofy, Pluto, Chip and Dale.

In Fantasyland, you can meet Anna, Elsa and Olaf at *Frozen Fantasy Gardens Village*. You can also meet Tinker Bell at *Fairy Tale Forest*.

In Toy Story Land, at *Barrel of Fun*, you can meet Woody, Jessie and Buzz.

In Adventureland, you can meet various Disney characters at *Karibuni Marketplace*. These change regularly but include Carl

and Russell from Up, King Louie and Baloo from The Jungle Book, Timon and Rafiki from The Lion King, Genie and Princess Jasmine from Aladdin, Judy and Nick from Zootopia, as well as Lilo and Stitch. Moana also has her own dedicated meeting spot in Adventureland.

Finally, in Tomorrowland, you can meet Iron Man at the *Iron Man Tech Showcase*, and BB-8, R2-D2 and Chewbacca at *Star Wars Command Post*. You may also find other characters such as Spider-Man meeting in this land.

Hotels:
Characters are present at all the Disney hotels, including throughout the day in the lobby and at various activities such as *Morning Movie Time with Goofy* at

Disney's Hollywood Hotel, *Explorers' Poolside Adventure* with a Disney character in the afternoon at Disney Explorers Lodge, and *Tai Chi with Master Goofy* in the morning at the Hong Kong Disneyland Hotel.

You can also meet characters when dining. Meet Mickey Mouse at *Chef Mickey* (Disney's Hollywood Hotel), various Disney characters at breakfast time at *World of Color Restaurant* (Disney Explorers Lodge) and Mickey and the gang at *Dragon Wind* (Disney Explorers Lodge). Finally, Hong Kong Disneyland Hotel's *Enchanted Garden Restaurant* offers meets with Disney characters as you enjoy a buffet meal.

Hong Kong Disneyland Park Guide

Hong Kong Disneyland is composed of seven lands filled with fantasy, adventure, and excitement.

The park is loosely based on the original Disneyland that opened in California in 1955, and up until recently even had the same Sleeping Beauty Castle as its centrepiece. Over the past 15 years, the park has expanded again and again, and now features unique areas such as Mystic Point and Grizzly Gulch which cannot be found in other Disney parks, as well as more well-known areas such as Fantasyland and Adventureland.

Hong Kong Disneyland is the 16th most visited theme park in the world. The park has plenty to offer guests with around 30 attractions (rides, themed areas, and shows), as well as character experiences, dining options, and an abundance of places to shop.

The park is divided into seven areas (or "lands") around the Castle of Magical Dreams in the centre. These are Main Street, U.S.A, Grizzly Gulch (the equivalent to Frontierland in other Disney parks), Mystic Point, Tomorrowland, Toy Story Land, Fantasyland, and Adventureland. Each land has its own overarching theme, with its own soundtrack, décor, costumes, and themed attractions.

We will now take a look at each land individually, as well as the attractions, dining options, and other notable features.

A Note on Wait Times:
Waiting in queue lines to get on rides is inevitable at theme parks. In our guide books, we typically include the usual wait time for rides, however, compared to other Disney parks, the wait times at Hong Kong Disneyland are practically non-existent, so we are not including these.

	Does the attraction have Fastpass?		Minimum height (in cm)
	Is there an On-Ride Photo?		Attraction Length

Main Street, U.S.A.

Main Street, U.S.A. is the entrance to Hong Kong Disneyland, taking you towards the Castle of Magical Dreams and beyond. This area of the park is themed to look like a 1920s American town.

Main Street contains many shops on both sides of the street, the king of which is the **Emporium** where you are sure to find something to buy!

There are many places to eat along the street too, including Quick Service and Table Service restaurants, as well as snack locations. There are also other food shops and carts around Main Street, U.S.A. too.

Before entering Main Street, U.S.A. itself, there is Town Square with a gazebo in the centre.

City Hall is immediately to your left on Town Square; this is "Guest Services". Ask

any questions you have here. They can also make reservations for tours and restaurants, and accept complaints and positive feedback too.

You will often find character meets in this area of the

park, as well as live music.

Top Tip: As you walk along Main Street, U.S.A., listen to the sounds from the windows on the first floor to hear the town's residents.

Hong Kong Disneyland Railroad – Main Street Station

Take a grand tour of Hong Kong Disneyland onboard an authentic steam train. Whether you use it as a form of transportation or just a way of seeing the sights, the Disneyland Railroad is a fun way to enjoy the park.

A full trip around the park takes about 15 minutes. There is an additional stop in Fantasyland.

This attraction usually ceases operation several hours before the park closes.

Animation Academy

Learn about how the Disney characters are brought to life at the Animation Academy through a show with a difference. Here, you can learn how to draw one of the characters for yourself and take your efforts home!

Main Street Vehicles

These vehicles travel up and down Main Street.

They typically only operate in the morning, and you simply wait for the next vehicle to turn up at designated spots.

Dining

Main Street Bakery – Quick Service/Snacks. Sells donuts, pastries, sandwiches, desserts, pizzas, as well as hot and cold drinks. Most individual items are HK$30-50. This is a good place to grab breakfast in the park.

Main Street Corner Café – Table Service. American and Chinese cuisine. Entrees include Japanese pork cutlet, Korean deep-fried chicken, Beyond burger, rib-eye steak and more with prices at HK$178-298. 3-course sets menu vary in price between HK$226-346. Children's meals are HK$112. Also serves a 2-person afternoon tea.

Market House – Quick Service/Snacks. Serves Starbucks coffee and other beverages. Most drinks are around $HK40.

Main Street Market – Outdoor vending cart. Serves Mickey waffles, ice cream and turkey legs. Most snacks are around HK$50.

Plaza Inn – Table Service. Serves Chinese cuisine such as dim sum and rice rolls at HK$72-98 per portion. Other entrees include poached chicken, barbecue pork, suckling pig, roasted goose, marinated chicken, lamb shanks and fish fillets (HK$178-360). Also offers set menus from HK$208.

You will also find a group of carts selling popcorn, ice cream, sandwiches and coffee.

Adventureland

Explore the wildest land at Hong Kong Disneyland where you can see the jungle and meet familiar Disney friends.

As well as the attractions listed in this section, Adventureland also houses **Karibuni Marketplace** where you can meet Disney characters, play games for prizes, and shop. You will also find a water spray area filled with leaky totem poles called **Liki Tikis** which is perfect to cool down in in the summer.

Rafts and Tarzan's Treehouse

Take a raft over to explore Tarzan's treehouse in this self-guided and relaxing attraction. You can get good photos of figures of Tarzan and Jane as you walk around.

Jungle River Cruise

Jump aboard and get ready to set sail through jungles across the world seeing the world's animals with fun animatronics, natives, and special effects. On the boat, there is a skipper who is there to entertain you.

You can choose to join one of three queues for a tour either in Mandarin, Cantonese or English – there is a boat for each language every 10 minutes and the boats alternate between the three languages.

Perhaps due to the language barrier, there is

less dry humour in this version of the Jungle River Cruise compared to the American Disney parks.

Although this ride takes place on water, you shouldn't get wet.

 No   📷 No   None   ⌄ 7 minutes

Festival of the Lion King

 No   📷 No   None   7 minutes

Festival of The Lion King is one of our favourite shows at Hong Kong Disneyland and a true celebration of the essence of The Lion King movies.

The show does not follow the film's storyline, but instead includes the best songs interpreted by professionals in an African-inspired setting. This is a definite must-do.

Moana: A Home-Coming Celebration

This is a unique retelling of the story of Moana including puppets, dancers and Moana herself. It is our least favourite permanent show at the park as it is so simple compared to the other shows, but it is a fun show none-the-less. Moana tells the story in English with other characters translating the story into Cantonese.

No · No · None · 20 minutes

The show takes place in an outdoor theatre which is not shaded with guests seating on bench-like seating. There is not an abundance of seating, so turn up at least 15 minutes if you want to sit down – alternatively, you can stand at the back or around the theatre.

Dining

River View Café – Quick Service/Snacks. Chinese cuisine. Offers a Moana-themed Asian snack set menu at HK$169 per guest. Also serves small plates such as chicken soup in a coconut (HK$59), yin yang fried rice (HK$149), custard buns and sesame buns (HK$39), as well as hot and cold drinks (HK$28-60).
Tahitian Terrace – Quick Service. Asian cuisine. Serves curry dishes with fish, beef, duck and vegetable options (HK$129-135). The kids meal of roasted chicken breast with rice is HK$95.

There is also an outdoor vending cart which sells Korean squid, turkey legs and ice cream, as well as a drinks vending machine.

Fantasyland

Find classic Disney attractions here, in this land dedicated to the youngest members of the family. Hong Kong Disneyland's gentle toddler-friendly rides are found here in the most magical of all the lands, and there is plenty of variety.

As well as the attractions listed in this section, you will also find **Fantasyland Station** on the Hong Kong Disneyland Railroad here.

Castle of Magical Dreams

Hong Kong Disneyland is currently going through a multi-year expansion and one of the most significant changes that all guests will see is the transformation of *Sleeping Beauty Castle* into the new *Castle of Magical Dreams* which will stand at more than twice the height and become a new landmark for the park. The castle's design pays tribute to 13 Disney princesses and heroines, including Moana for the very first time.

Once the castle opens guests will once again be able to walk through the castle to reach Fantasyland. Guests will also be able to **meet princesses** inside the castle, and fairy-godmothers-in-training will turn young girls into princesses with makeovers, hair styling and special outfits in a new **Bibbidi Bobbidi Boutique** location, just like the one at Hong Kong Disneyland hotel.

The castle will also feature a new stage at the front which will host daytime shows with a dedicated staggered viewing area for guests. The fountains in the castle moat will also feature in the park's new nighttime spectacular.

The castle is set to be unveiled on 1st July 2020, although as of April 2020 HK Disneyland is closed due to a worldwide pandemic so there may be a delay to this opening date.

Mickey's PhilharMagic

PhilharMagic is a fun 4D show, and in our opinion, one that should not be missed.

 No   No   None   9 minutes

The story is that you are attending Goofy's opera performance with Mickey's Philharmonic orchestra. When Donald gets involved, however, things get a little out of hand, and you end up on an adventure travelling through a world of Disney classics. Do not miss this fun show.

With an air-conditioned queue line and theatre, shelter from the rain, and a mash-up of Disney's greatest hit songs, this is worth stopping by to watch.

The audio for this show, including all dialogue and songs, is in English.

Top Tip: At the show's conclusion, when Donald flies off the screen, and the curtain goes down, look at the back of the theatre for an extra special surprise.

Dumbo The Flying Elephant

Step aboard and fly through the skies with Dumbo!

Situated right in the centre of Fantasyland, it offers great views of the surrounding area, as well as being a whole lot of fun. At the fof each Dumbo elephant, there is a lever that allows you to lift your Dumbo up or down into the air!

| | No | | No | | None | | 1 minute 30 seconds |

Due to its popularity, its slow loading nature and low hourly capacity, Dumbo can have waits of 15 minutes when the rest of Fantasyland has no waits at all.

Cinderella Carousel

This is a beautiful vintage-style carousel that is sure to create memories for guests of all ages. This truly is a ride for every member of the family.

Located in front of the carousel is the Sword in the Stone. Try pulling it out, and if you are the right person for the job and you get the sword out, you might just be crowned King or Queen of the kingdom!

| | No | | No | | None | | 2 minutes |

Fairy Tale Forest

This walkthrough attraction features miniature scenes from popular Disney movies such as Tangled Cinderella, and Beauty and the Beast.

At certain times of the day, you can also meet Tinker Bell inside the *Fairy Tale Forest*. This is an optional meet.

It takes about 5 to 10 minutes to walk through the *Fairy Tale Forest*.

The Many Adventures of Winnie the Pooh

Hop inside one of Pooh's honey pots and find out what it is like to step through the page into one his many adventures – you can expect to see Pooh bear, Tigger, Eeyore, Piglet and other friends.

This is a slow, gentle ride through the stories of Winnie the Pooh. The ride itself is filled with bright colours that should excite the little ones. It is one of the more elaborate rides in Fantasyland and great fun.

FP Yes | 📷 Yes | None | 3 minutes 30 seconds

This is one of two rides in the park to have Fastpass, so use it if the wait is long.

"it's a small world"

One of the most memorable and popular park attractions, *"it's a small world"* features hundreds of dolls singing a catchy tune about the uniting of the world.

As your boat sails leisurely through the attraction, you can enjoy sights and sounds from around the world.

The loading system is efficient, meaning that the number of people who can enjoy the ride every hour is high; this means wait times are usually very low, and there is a continually moving queue line. This is a

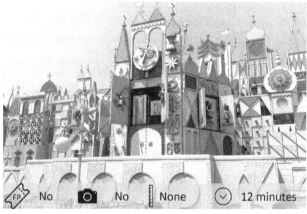

FP No | 📷 No | None | 12 minutes

great Disney classic that, although not based on any film franchise, is a "must-do" for most visitors.

Top Tip: Look for the dolls that look like Disney characters such as Aladdin and Woody.

Mad Hatter Tea Cups

Hop inside one of the teacups from Alice in Wonderland and start spinning wildly.

The ride functions much like any other teacup ride around the world, where you have a wheel at the centre of the cup and you can turn it to spin yourself around faster, or leave it alone and have a more relaxing spin.

FP — No   📷 No   None   🕐 1 minute 30 seconds

Mickey and the Wondrous Book

Journey into an enchanted storybook with Mickey and Goofy as Disney movies come to life on stage in front of your very eyes.

When the book opens you see scenes and hear songs from The Jungle Book, Little Mermaid, Tangled, Brave, Frozen, Aladdin, and Princess and the Frog. The show uses a clever mix of projections, screens, real sets, characters, fantastic live singers and dancers. This is a must-see show.

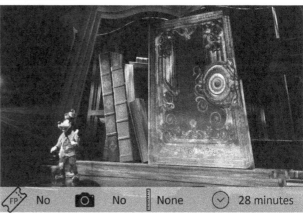

FP — No   📷 No   None   🕐 28 minutes

The show dialogue is performed in Cantonese with the music in English. Screens to the left and right of the stage translate the character dialogue into Simplified Chinese and English.

Arrive about 20 minutes ahead of the show start time during off-peak, and 30 minutes at peak times to get a good seat.

Dining

Royal Banquet Hall – Quick Service. Serves 4 types of cuisine: Grill, Japanese, Guang Dong, and International. Serves steak, chicken, fish, pork bone ramen, Japanese curry, sushi, seafood fried rice, steamed chicken, steamed pork ribs, baked pork chop, pork Bolognese, Hawaiian pizza, vegetarian options and more. Entrees are HK$132-149. Dim sum is HK$38 per portion. Kids meals are HK$99. This is one of our recommended restaurants to dine at with a wide variety of choices.

Clopin's Festival of Foods – Quick Service. Serves Chinese cuisine such as regional noodles, Guangdong BBQ, and kung pao chicken and braised pork. Entrees are HK$125-129. Kids meals are HK$95.

Small World Ice Cream – Snacks. Serves ice cream and waffle baskets with fruit.

There are also two outdoor carts in this area. One serves popcorn and ice creams, the other serves soya chicken legs, corn on the cob, jumbo hot dogs, and ice creams.

Tomorrowland

Step into the land of tomorrow as you take a peek into the future.

As well as the attractions listed in this section, you will also find **Star Wars: Command Post** in this area where you can meet Star Wars characters including R2-D2 and Chewbacca, and **Iron Man: Tech Showcase** where you can meet Iron Man.

Hyperspace Mountain

Space Mountain is a rollercoaster through space designed with the family in mind - it has no loops or inversions and recreates the feeling of soaring through the galactic world.

We strongly recommend a Fastpass if the wait is long as the queue line is not well-themed and ends up feeling even longer than it really is.

Note that this ride is tamer than its Walt Disney World counterpart, and much tamer than the Disneyland Paris version. It is very similar to the Disneyland (California) version.

FP✓ Yes   📷 Yes   📏 102cm   ⌄ 2 minutes 30 seconds

Note: This attraction has been temporarily transformed into 'Hyperspace Mountain' with a re-themed interior featuring new audio and projections from the Star Wars universe. There is no announced end date for this 'temporary' experience.

Orbitron

Soar above Tomorrowland in your very own flying saucer.

This is a spinning-type ride similar to *Dumbo* in Fantasyland where you

 No   No   None   1 minute 30 seconds

control how high you go.

It is a lot of fun but we would not say it is a must-

do, because of the similarity to other attractions such as *Dumbo* – it does, however, usually have a shorter wait.

Jedi Training – Trials of the Temple

Show Length: 15 minutes

For the younger adventurers, this is the chance to get up on stage and yield a lightsaber and battle the dark side.

Unfortunately for adults, only children can participate in the experience and take part in the show. For those not participating, the show is still entertaining to watch.

The show is a mix of Cantonese and English.

Jedi Training takes place several times per day. Consult your park Times Guide for showtimes.

Ant-Man and The Wasp: Nano Battle!

Help Ant-Man and The Wasp defeat enemy Zola's bots in this interactive ride.

As you move from scene to scene, you score points by hitting the targets on the bots with your blasters—targets are worth different amounts, so look at the signs in the queue for an explanation of which are worth more.

If you have visited other Disney parks, this is an upgraded, newer version of the Buzz Lightyear shooting ride. The technology used

FP: No   📷 No   None   ✓ 4 minutes 30 seconds

here, though, makes for a more fun and accurate game.

This is the newest attraction in the park (opened March 2019).

Iron Man Experience

Iron Man Experience is a 3D simulator-style ride where you join Tony Stark from Stark Enterprises aboard an Iron Wing to tour Hong Kong from the skies and see the newly completed Stark Tower. However, things don't go according to plan and Stark must put on his Iron Man suit to save the day.

If you have visited other Disney parks before, this is a newer upgraded version of the *Star Tours* ride system.

This is a fun ride, but those

FP: No   📷 No   None   ✓ 2 minutes

prone to motion sickness should avoid it – or ask to sit

at the front row where there is less movement.

Dining

Comet Café – Quick Service. Serves Chinese cuisine. Dishes include wok classics such as roasted eel, braised park or omni minced pork, as well as noodles with flavours including seafood, beef and pork. Entrees are HK$119-139. This restaurant is entirely outdoors and although it has shaded seating, you may prefer to visit Starliner Diner for the air-con.
Starliner Diner – Quick Service. Serves Western cuisine (the only Quick Service location dedicated to this in the park). Dishes include beef burgers, fish nuggets, fried chicken and veggie burgers. Entrees are HK$109-119. A kids mushroom and chicken burger meal is HK$85. Also serves hot and cold drinks (including fresh fruit juice), desserts and sides such as chicken wings.
BB-8 Snack Cart – Snacks. Sells drinks and ice creams.

There is also an outdoor vending cart which sells popcorn, cotton candy and ice creams.

Toy Story Land

Toy Story Land shrinks you down to the size of a toy in Andy's back yard.

All the rides in Toy Story Land only welcome a small number of guests each hour. Due to this, waits for all rides here are often some of the longest in the park. Therefore, we recommend visiting Toy Story Land early in the day, making it the first thing, if possible.

As well as the attractions listed in this section, you can meet characters at **Barrel of Fun**.

RC Racer

Hop on the RC car from Pixar's Toy Story films, and feel the wind in your hair as you ride both forwards and backwards in the car.

The ride is great fun and a good adrenaline rush – it is often likened to the swinging pirate ships found at many theme parks, but we prefer the feeling on this. Here, you are also secured by harnesses, which you aren't on a pirate ship.

FP: No   Photo: No   120cm   1 minute

At the highest point, riders are 24m (80ft) high, and the free-fall feeling backwards is great fun.

The ride looks significantly more intimidating than it actually is and the sensation is not anywhere near as scary as it seems, in our opinion.

RC Racer has one of the most boring, and tedious, queues in all the park so we would recommend avoiding it if waits are long; the queue also moves very slowly.

Toy Soldier Parachute Drop

Fastpass: No
Minimum Height: 81cm
On-ride Photo: No
Ride Length: 1 min 15 secs

Board one of the Toy

Soldiers' parachutes and get ready to soar up into the sky and then glide back down to the ground again and again.

This is a great family ride and has become a new rite of passage for many.

Queues can get long for this ride, so we recommend doing this early in the day.

Slinky Dog Spin

Fastpass: No
Minimum Height: None
On-ride Photo: No
Ride Length: 1 minute 10 seconds

Hop on Slinky Dog and enjoy yourself as you spin around and around in circles getting increasingly faster and faster.

This is a fun family-friendly attraction that is likely to entertain everyone from young toddlers to parents.

Dining
Jessie's Snack Roundup – Snacks. Sells soft serve ice creams, churros, fruit cups & drinks.

Grizzly Gulch

Grizzly Gulch is Hong Kong Disneyland's answer to Frontierland.

Grizzly Gulch is dominated by a runaway mine car attraction, and also features plenty of photo opportunities, as well as **Geyser Gulch** a water play area for all ages.

Big Grizzly Mountain Runaway Mine Cars

Big Grizzly Mountain Runaway Mine Cars is Hong Kong Disneyland's most thrilling attraction.

This is a roller coaster ride where you hop on a mine-cart to explore the mountain. When the mine cart's chain breaks you find out that this isn't just any normal coaster though – expect to go forwards, backwards and reach speeds of 56km/h.

This is a fun family coaster and is a must-do in the park.

| FP | No | 📷 No | 112cm | ⏱ 3 minutes |

Dining

Lucky Nugget Saloon – Quick Service. Serves chicken nuggets, fish and chips and Caesar salad. This restaurant does not offer any indoor seating.

There are also two outdoor carts in this area. One sells popcorn, the other sells ice creams.

Mystic Point

Mystic Point is Hong Kong Disneyland's newest land, having opened in Summer 2013. It features the park's version of the Disney classic Haunted Mansion as an all-new attraction, Mystic Manor.

There are also two other minor attractions in Mystic Point. **Mystic Point Freight Depot** is a walkthrough area with large artefacts from Lord Henry Mystic's collection – good for photos. **Garden of Wonders** is also a walkthrough area where you can look through viewfinders and see illusions.

Mystic Manor

Mystic Manor is a trackless dark ride which takes you into the amazing collection of artefacts collected by Lord Henry Mystic. When his pet monkey, Albert, touches the beautifully carved magic box, the museum comes to life. It really has to be seen to be believed – Disney has truly outdone itself with this ride.

This is perhaps the best ride in the resort and it is suitable for all ages, although the ride may be a little loud for the very youngest of adventurers.

FP: No   📷 No   None   ⊘ 5 minutes 30 seconds

Dining

Explorers Club Restaurant – Quick Service. Serves Asian and halal options. Entrees include nasi goreng, seafood noodles, butter chicken masala, black lentils, ginseng chicken soup, Korean beef, shabu shabu and more. Entrees cost HK$129-165. Kids meals are HK$99. This is a fantastic restaurant and one of our recommended places to eat.

There is also an outdoor ice cream cart opposite Mystic Manor.

Park Entertainment

Flights of Fantasy Parade

Parade Length: 10 minutes

Flights of Fantasy is the best way to see all your favourite Disney characters in one place as they parade down Main Street, U.S.A., around the park's hub and end near *Space Mountain*. The daytime Disney parade is one of the main events in any guest's Disney park day!

The parade is performed daily and the time varies seasonally. Check the app or Times Guide for the exact schedule.

Characters in the parade may vary from day to day but you can typically see about 25 different characters and floats, including: Pluto, Donald, Mickey, Minnie, Goofy, Chip 'n Dale, Belle, Cinderella, Snow White, Aurora, Baloo, King Louie, Rafiki, Timon, Tinker Bell, Lilo and Stitch, Jessie, the Green Army Men, Buzz, Woody, Winnie the Pooh, Tigger, and Eeyore. Unfortunately, the parade does not feature any of the newer film characters such as those from Frozen and Zootopia, and is shorter than most Disney parades – but, it's still a must-see.

It is not just the characters that are exciting though, the floats are amazing too. The soundtrack is a mix of English and Cantonese, and the whole event is even kicked off with a marching band! Plus, you can get involved in the parade by playing games as part of the parade's show stop.

The most popular place to watch the parade is along Main Street, U.S.A. You should secure your spot about 20 to 30 minutes before the parade starts for the best view if watching from here. Elsewhere, especially closer to Tomorrowland, you can turn up later.

The parade is not cancelled during light or moderate rain. During heavy rain, or if there is a thunderstorm alert, there is the potential for the parade to be cancelled or delayed. In either case, an announcement will be made at the parade start time.

Pixar Water Play Street Party!

Parade Length: 20 minutes

In the summer, Hong Kong Disneyland presents an additional parade and party where the aim is to get guests wet as they see the Incredibles, as well as characters from Onward, Inside Out, Up and Finding Nemo dance away.

You will want a front-row spot for this parade as guest umbrellas will block the view if you are any further back. You will get very wet! Watch the show on Main Street, U.S.A.

Paint the Night Parade

Parade Length: 20 minutes

This has very quickly become our favourite nighttime parade at any Disney park, and is one of the best nighttime spectaculars too.

Paint the Night features innovative floats, catchy tunes, dancers and many of your favourite characters. It truly is one of those parades that has to be seen to be believed.

During the parade, you can see Tinker Bell, Peter Pan, Sulley and Mike (from Monster's Inc.), Lightning McQueen, Ariel, Sebastian, Flounder, Nemo, Jessie,

Woody, Buzz Lightyear, Belle, Rapunzel, Cinderella, Anna and Elsa, Olaf, Goofy, Donald, Minnie and Mickey.

Paint the Night is performed

nightly for most of the year – check the park times guide or app for performance times.

We Love Mickey Projection Show

Show Length: 10 minutes

The 'We Love Mickey' show is a psychedelic over the top projection show all about Mickey Mouse and his cartoons.

The show is projected onto the buildings on Main Street, U.S.A each evening. Mickey Mouse also comes out dancing on a float at the end.

If you want the best view of the float, stand at the end of Main Street on the corner with Town Square.

It is not a must-see in our opinion, but it is often timed around *Paint the Night* parade so if it is only a short time between them, watch both – you can turn up just as the show starts. There is no need to be there in advance.

The show was introduced in 2018 when *Sleeping Beauty Castle* closed for its transformation into the *Castle of Magical Dreams*. When the new castle is unveiled in Summer 2020, we expect this show to end and be replaced by a vastly superior nighttime spectacular on the new castle which includes music, projections, fireworks, fountains and other special effects.

Dining

There are a variety of places to eat at Hong Kong Disneyland. Food options vary from sandwich and snack locations to Quick Service (fast food) places, character buffets, Table Service dining and even fine dining options. Eating can be as much a part of the experience as the attractions at Hong Kong Disneyland.

Making Reservations

If you want to dine at a specific Table Service or Buffet restaurant, it is worth booking a table in advance. Disney calls its reservations 'Priority Seating'.

With a Disney hotel reservation, you can make your restaurant either in advance or at the resort.

You can call +852 3550-3388. Reservations can be made up to 42 days before your visit - or 120 days before your arrival date if staying at the Disney hotels.

The restaurants also take walk-ins and same-day reservations if available.

There is no option to pre-purchase dining plans or meal credits. Each restaurant is paid for at the restaurant when dining.

Top Tip: If you wish to dine at *Enchanted Garden Restaurant*, specifically, it is worth booking in advance - it is popular.

Restaurant Types

Buffet – All-you-can-eat locations where you fill your plate from the food selection as many times as you want. Buffets may or may not include drinks.

Quick Service – Fast food. Look at the menus, pay for your food and collect it a few minutes later. You will find everything from burgers and chips, to chicken, to pizza and pasta.

Most of the restaurants at the resort are Quick Service.

Table Service – Order from a menu. You are served by a waiter who brings your food to your table.

Character Buffets – These are available all day and are all-you-can-eat places where characters interact with you and take photos as you eat.

Top Tip: You usually do not have to order from a set menu. Ordering specific items 'a la carte' is fine.

Top Tip 2: The 'set meals' at Hong Kong Disneyland Quick Service locations are referred to as "combos", so if you just want a burger which is in a set meal ask the Cast Member for "burger only – no combo" to make it clear.

Snacks

A huge part of Disney and theme park culture is snacks, especially snacks that look cute. You may well find that you can skip a meal and eat snacks instead.

Some of the most popular:
• **Mickey Waffles** – A Disney classic. Sold at the waffle cart on Main Street, U.S.A
• **Dim-Sum** – Find this at

Royal Banquet Hall in Fantasyland.
• **Sweet treats and Pastries** – Everything from Donald and Pooh donuts to pineapple bread to egg tarts. Sold at Main Street Bakery on Main Street USA.
• **Mickey Ice Cream Bar** – Sold in carts throughout the park. Hong Kong Disneyland also has an exclusive

Strawberry and chocolate flavoured Minnie Ice Cream Bar.
• **Fried Squid** – Perhaps the most unique and 'local' snack item in the park. Sold at a cart in Adventureland.
• **Popcorn** – Sold throughout the park from carts in a variety of flavours including steak, strawberry and caramel.

Touring Plan

A touring plan is an easy-to-follow guide that minimises your waiting time in queue lines throughout the day. By following this, you can maximise your time in the park and experience more attractions.

To see all of Hong Kong Disneyland, you need one day. However, you can hit the headline attractions at the park in less time.

This touring plan is not set in stone, so feel free to adapt it to the needs of your party. It is important to note that the plan focuses on experiencing the rides; if your focus is on meeting all the characters or seeing all the shows, a touring plan is unlikely to be suitable. The only way to minimise waits for characters is to get to the parks and the meet-and-greets early – these often have longer wait times than the rides.

If you do not want to experience a particular ride, skip that step but do not change the order of the steps. If an attraction is closed for refurbishment during your trip, skip that step.

Purchase your tickets in advance to save time. If you need to buy a ticket on the day, turn up 20 minutes earlier than the start times on these plans - and even earlier during peak season.

1 Day Plan

Arrive at the park entrance about 40 minutes before the park's scheduled opening time if you are planning on meeting characters – the park opens Town Square up until the entrance of Main Street, U.S.A. 30 minutes earlier than the advertised park opening time.

If you don't want to meet any characters, arrive at the park 15 minutes before the opening time to give you time to get through security and walk to the roped off area of Main Street, U.S.A.

Note: Hong Kong Disneyland often closes either Tomorrowland, or Grizzly Gulch and Mystic Point early in the evening during quieter periods. Use the app, Times Guide, look out for signs at the entrance of these lands or ask a Cast Member to check which land(s) closes early on that day. This plan assumes that Tomorrowland closes early, so it saves the Grizzly Gulch and Mystic

Point attractions for the evening. If those two lands are closing early instead, follow the plan below up to (and including) riding *Jungle River Cruise*, then visit Grizzly Gulch and Mystic Point, followed by Fantasyland and end in Tomorrowland. When HK Disneyland launches its new nighttime spectacular in 2020, Fantasyland may close early instead – in this case, follow the plan as normal.

Morning:
• Head to Toy Story Land. This land is filled with low capacity attractions, which can often get longer waits than the rest of the park. Ride *RC Racer* first, then *Slinky Dog Spin*, then *Toy Soldier Parachute Drop*.
• Go to Adventureland. Ride *Jungle River Cruise*.
• Go to Tomorrowland. Ride *Iron Man Experience*.
• Ride *Ant-Man and the Wasp*.
• Grab a Fastpass for *Space Mountain*.

• Head to Fantasyland. Grab lunch at Royal Banquet Hall.

Afternoon:
• Watch *Mickey and the Wondrous Book*.
• Ride *"it's a small world"*
• Watch the daytime parade
• Use your *Space Mountain* Fastpass around this plan. Get a *The Many Adventures of Winnie the Pooh* Fastpass as soon as you can.
• Ride *Dumbo the Flying Elephant* and watch *Mickey's PhilharMagic*.
• Ride *Cinderella Carousel* and *Mad Hatter Teacups*.

Evening:
• Head to Adventureland to watch *Festival of the Lion King*.
• Ride *Big Grizzly Mountain Runaway Mine Cars*.
• Ride *Mystic Manor*.
• Have dinner at Explorer's Club Restaurant.
• Get a spot for *Paint the Night* or another nighttime spectacular 20-30 minutes before the start time.

Outside the Park

Unlike every other Disney resort in the world, Hong Kong Disneyland does not have a 'Downtown Disney' dining and entertainment street or area outside the theme park. The only attraction near the park is Inspiration Lake, and a little further away you have the Tian Tan Buddha (Big Buddha).

Inspiration Lake

Inspiration Lake is a Disney-made lake which opened in 2005 to act as a recreation centre and irrigation reservoir for the resort.

At the lake, there is a 7-Eleven convenience store with a recreation centre offering a boat and surrey bike rental service, a playground, a 1.5km running track and picturesque waterfalls. This is definitely not a must-do, but if you want a spot of nature in the middle of a day at the theme park, this is a good place to come.

The lake is serene but, unfortunately, the sounds of nature are interrupted every couple of minutes by a plane landing into Hong Kong International Airport only a few miles away. The lake area is open daily from 9:00am to 7:00pm – there is no admission cost. The shop is open from 9:30am to 6:45pm, and the recreation centre operates between 10:00am and 5:00pm.

Reach Inspiration Lake with a 15 to 25-minute walk from the Disney hotels, a 15-minute stroll from the Disneyland Resort MTR station, or 20 minutes' walk from the theme park. You can also catch the public R8 bus from Disneyland Resort's central bus station (3-minute journey, runs every 20 minutes – payable with exact change or Octopus card). You can also drive and park at Inspiration Lake (parking fees apply).

Tian Tan Buddha (Big Buddha)

The Big Buddha is rated as the third best thing to see in Hong Kong according to TripAdvisor ratings. The most hassle-free way to reach this iconic sight is to take a 40-minute taxi ride to the Buddha, but that is also the most boring way.

For a more adventurous trip, you want to reach Tung Chung station by the airport. Take the MTR Disney Resort Line to Sunny Bay station (1 stop) and then the Tung Chung line

one stop to Tung Chung.

At Tung Chung, you can take a 25-minute cable car ride through lush scenery to the peak on Ngong Ping 360, or the 23 public bus. Both drop you off at Ngong Ping Village (which is to be honest, a tourist trap) – here you can walk to the Big Buddha.

On the way back, at Tung Chung, you can stop at the mall or fashion outlet if you'd like.

Guests with Disabilities

This section covers procedures and accommodations Disney makes for guests visiting with disabilities. It includes people with mobility, hearing and visual impairments. If you are familiar with the Disability Access Service at other Disney parks which allows faster entry or timed entry into attractions, note that this is not available at Hong Kong Disneyland.

Dedicated parade viewing areas are available for guests with disabilities and their party on a first-come-first-served basis. For a full detailed list of individual attraction disability accommodations, see Disney's guide at www.bit.ly/hkdisab.

Mobility

Hong Kong Disneyland strives to allow all guests to utilise the main attraction entrances whenever possible, allowing the ride queuing system to be as equal as possible for all guests, whatever their physical or mental abilities. All park toilets are accessible too.

However, accessibility does vary from attraction to attraction within the Disney Parks – disabled guests should ask a Cast Member at the entrance to an attraction for the appropriate entrance. Sometimes guests can ride in their own wheelchairs, and other times they must transfer to a ride vehicle.

The daily cost of hiring a wheelchair is HK$60, or HK$30 for seniors (ages 65 and over). A refundable deposit of HK$100 per day is required. The rental location is at the firehouse to the right of City Hall on Main Street, U.S.A. The Disney hotels also have a wheelchair rental service that can also be used from the hotel to the park, as well as inside the theme park itself.

You are, of course, welcome to bring your own stroller or wheelchair if you wish.

An accessible resort shuttle is available for guests between the hotels and the theme park; speak to a Cast Member to request it.

Hearing

Guests with hearing disabilities have access to Assistive Listening Systems which use a receiver to amplify sound and are recommended for guests with mild to moderate hearing loss.
This service is available at *Festival of the Lion King* and *Mickey's PhilharMagic*.

There are also written aids in the form of Guest Assistance Packets containing attraction dialogue and narration, a flashlight, and a pencil and paper. These are available at Guest Relations in City Hall on Main Street, U.S.A. No deposit is required.

Sign language interpretation is also available at some live shows (*Festival of the Lion King, Jungle River Cruise* and *Mickey and the Wondrous Book*) with a minimum of 7-day notice—at no extra charge. E-mail guest@hongkongdisneyland.com to request this.

Visual

Guests with visual disabilities have the following accommodations for them at the theme parks: Braille guidebooks, audio guides, and stationary tactile maps. The maps are available in both English and Chinese. Service dogs are also permitted in the theme park, but are not permitted on certain attractions. Dedicated backstage 'relief' areas are available – ask a Cast Member for details.

Hong Kong Disneyland for Disney Park Veterans

Many guests visit Hong Kong Disneyland after having visited another Disney theme park. Here we compare Hong Kong Disneyland with the other Disney theme parks, including the Walt Disney World Resort in Florida, the Disneyland Resort in California, Disneyland Paris, Shanghai Disneyland and Tokyo Disneyland.

Local Customs, Language & Park Etiquette

Hong Kong is often described as where East meets West, and Hong Kong Disneyland is a perfect example of this. It is important to remember that Hong Kong was under the rule of the British until 1997. At the moment it is part of the "One China, Two Systems" policy which means it has its own government, laws and autonomy – Hong Kong has, however, become increasingly Chinese as the years have passed.

Hong Kong Disneyland is most similar to Walt Disney World in this respect – it has local visitors which account for around 75% of guests, with 25% being foreign. At the US parks, this figure is 18-22% and at Disneyland Paris around 50% of guests are foreign.

The international nature of Hong Kong Disneyland and the historical British rule mean that English is not a language barrier here, in the same was way as it is not a language barrier in Disneyland Paris. All shows are translated into both Cantonese and English. This means travelling to HK Disneyland for English speakers is significantly easier than travelling to the Tokyo Disney Resort or Shanghai Disney Resort – English will be perfectly fine everywhere.

In terms of theme park etiquette, we find that (generally speaking) the visitors at Hong Kong Disneyland are significantly better behaved than those ay Shanghai Disneyland – we have not found a lack of personal space here, unlike at Shanghai. Nothing will ever match the orderly nature of Tokyo's guests, though.

We find the level of service of Cast Members throughout the resort to be on a par with Disney's excellent service worldwide – Tokyo still has a slight advantage here, however.

Logistics, Fastpass, Resort Size and Transportation

Hong Kong Disneyland will probably be the least stressful Disney park visit you will ever have – the resort is tiny compared to the others: there is only one theme park, and three on-site hotels. The theme park also doesn't reach anywhere near the level of crowding seen at other Disney resorts, and transport-wise the theme park is extremely well-connected.

Fastpass is only available on two rides at Hong Kong Disneyland – it uses the paper Fastpass system like at Disneyland Paris and Disneyland. There is no option of mobile digital Fastpass like at Walt Disney World.

In terms of size, the theme park itself – Hong Kong Disneyland – is only about 70 acres including the 2021 Frozen expansion and all the woodland areas. Every other Disney theme park is larger than this, with the largest three (Shanghai, Disneyland Park in Paris and Magic Kingdom) all coming in at over 100 acres – that's 40% more theme park land.

In this way, Hong Kong Disneyland feels very much like Disneyland Paris on a smaller scale as you can walk to everywhere on-site in under 20 minutes. It is also similar to Disneyland Resort in California in this respect, but California is landlocked whereas Hong Kong Disneyland has plenty of room to grow, making this resort more similar to Disneyland Paris and Shanghai Disneyland. Walt Disney World is, of course, sprawling.

Hong Kong Disneyland is also exceptionally well-connected to public transport with its own MTR train station – just like Tokyo, Shanghai and Paris. This can't be said for Disneyland or Walt Disney World.

Pricing

Hotels
At Hong Kong Disneyland, a standard room goes from HK$1980 ($255) to HS$4,235 ($435) depending on the season.

In comparison, at Shanghai Disney Resort rooms at Toy Story Hotel vary from ¥1,500 ($215) to ¥2,400 ($340) and at the Shanghai Disneyland Hotel, range from about ¥3,000 ($425) to ¥4,300 ($610).

The Disneyland Hotel at Disneyland Resort (the cheapest onsite hotel) costs $210 to $350 per night. The grandest, the Grand Californian has room rates at $475 to $980.

At Walt Disney World, you can expect to pay $154 to $316 for a value-level room at Pop Century Resort. A room goes from $425 to $846 at the deluxe-level Beach Club Resort.

At Tokyo Disney Resort, the cheapest room at a Value hotel (Tokyo Disney Celebration Hotel) starts at around ¥18,000 ($165) during low season per night. For a Deluxe hotel, you can pay ¥30,000 ($270) to ¥50,000 ($450) in the low season, depending on which hotel you choose.

Overall here, prices for the high-level resorts are very good value at Hong Kong Disneyland, particularly in low season when comparing to the other resorts. Even in high season, they are good value in comparison. Sadly, there is a lack of 'value' level hotels for those on a stricter budget at Hong Kong Disneyland – these guests have no option but to stay off-site.

Tickets
Hong Kong Disneyland's park tickets cost HK$639 (US$82) for adults and HK$475 (US$61). Park tickets do not vary in price according to season. This is roughly on a par with the average Shanghai Disneyland ticket in mid-season (¥399 [$56] to ¥699 [$99]).

A one-day entry ticket to Tokyo Disney Resort for one park is ¥7,500 ($69) for adults and ¥4,900 ($45) for children, which is cheaper than at Hong Kong.

For comparison, at Walt Disney World, a 1-day, 1-park adult ticket is $116 to $169 with tax. At Disneyland, it is $104 to $154.

A one-day entry ticket to Disneyland Paris for one park is €87 ($98) for adults and €80 for children – although there are big discounts of 30%+ by booking in advance.

As we can see above, park tickets at all the Asian parks

are significantly cheaper than in the US, but on average, HK Disneyland has the most expensive park tickets in Asia – considering it offers the least number of attractions, it is probably the least best-value Disney park in the world in terms of park ticket prices. No-one can beat Hong Kong Disneyland's HK$100 (US$13) senior ticket, however!

It is worth noting that you can get a discount on the HK ticket prices by buying through Klook.com (see our tickets chapter) and can get a discounted meal voucher to boot. You can also see the whole park in one day here, whereas realistically you need longer to cover the other parks.

Food

At Hong Kong Disneyland, a bottled drink is around US$3-4, putting it on a par with Tokyo. In the US parks and Disneyland Paris, a bottle of water or a Coke is $4. At Shanghai, these are $1-$2.50 each.

Food in Hong Kong Disneyland is similar to that in the US where a Quick Service meal with a drink is about $16. In Shanghai, this is about $14, and about $11 in Tokyo. Paris meals are on average the most expensive at around $17.

Snacks are roughly comparable in price at US$4-$6 at all the Disney parks.

Unique Attractions and Details

Hong Kong Disneyland has several unique rides and shows which cannot be found at the American Disney Parks, but most of the park will feel familiar to visitors of other Disney Parks. Hong Kong Disneyland particularly excels in its entertainment offering.

Main Street, U.S.A. is very similar to the one in Disneyland Resort, with no unique attractions.

Adventureland features *Jungle River Cruise* which is similar to the American and Japanese versions, but unique enough that it is worth seeing. *Festival of the Lion King* shares a name with a Walt Disney World show and the concept is similar, but the show is completely different.

Grizzly Gulch does not exist in other Disney parks. *Big Grizzly Mountain Runaway Mine Cars* is a mix of *Expedition Everest, TRON*'s launch and *Big Thunder Mountain* - it is a great fun, unique ride.

Mystic Point has the fantastic *Mystic Manor* which is unlike any other Disney dark ride and very different to the other *Haunted Mansion* attractions. The Explorer's Club Restaurant here is almost an attraction unto itself too.

Toy Story Land is a complete clone of Disneyland Paris' Toy Story Playland with a slightly different layout. It is also fairly similar to the land in Shanghai, but very different to Toy Story Land in Walt Disney World.

Fantasyland is filled with clones of Disney classics. Unique attractions include *Fairy Tale Forest* and the fantastic *Mickey and the Wondrous Book* live show.

Finally, Tomorrowland will feel familiar to most Disney parks visitors. It does, however, have the unique *Iron Man Experience*, and *Ant-Man and the Wasp: Nano Battle!* Both are worth experiencing as they are great rides, although they are essentially modern versions of *Star Tours* and *Buzz Lightyear* with a different theme.

The night-time parade *Paint the Night* can be seen at Disneyland in California, but the *We Love Mickey* projection show and the daytime parade are unique to the park.

Hong Kong Disneyland offers its guests something different throughout the year, with seasonal and special events that celebrate events such as Chinese New Year, Halloween and Christmas. This section explores all of these. Then, we take a look at the future of the resort.

9th January to 9th February 2020

Celebrate the Year of the Rat (or the Year of the Mouse as Disney calls it) with Mickey Mouse!

Along Main Street USA you will see festive decorations, including *fai chun*, beautiful lanterns and flowers. Mickey and his friends don Chinese New Year outfits and the Disneyland Band performs a series of CNY-themed songs!

2020 also features the specially created "Mickey's Lucky Trail" with nine spots in the park filled with good luck to help guests collect blessings for the new year. Guests can also collect the special edition set of two Mickey and Minnie stickers along the trail.

A Chinese New Year-edition of the "We Love Mickey!" Projection Show every

evening features Mickey dressed in a Chinese New Year outfit! Guests can also say "Kung Hei Fat Choi" to God of Fortune Goofy at The Annex and take photos with him for extra good luck!

Of the three main seasonal events, this is the 'lightest' in new entertainment. Everything is included with standard park admission.

Mid-September to 31st October

Halloween is Hong Kong Disneyland's most elaborate yearly celebration. Details vary slightly each year and all the entertainment is included with standard park admission.

Mickey, Minnie and the whole gang have prepared their favourite Halloween costumes, to welcome everyone. You can also meet Halloween-only characters such as Jack Skellington too.

As well as the standard daytime parade, there is an extra short parade called *Mickey's Halloween Time Street Party* for guests to enjoy with plenty of pumpkins and characters in

fun costumes.

Throughout the day in Adventureland, *Festival of the Lion King* is substituted by the fantastic *Let's Get Wicked* show, which is one of the highlights of the season.

There are also limited-edition merchandise and food and drink offerings for Halloween.

In the evening, a new stage show concludes the night called *Jack Skellington's Villainous Gathering*.

A Disney Christmas

Mid-November to 1st January

Celebrate the most wonderful time of the year at Hong Kong Disneyland.

Details vary slightly each year and all the entertainment is included with standard park admission.

Mickey, Minnie and the whole gang are dressed in their festive best. At The Annex, you can meet Santa Mickey, and at Comet Café you can hello to Santa Stitch.

The *Mickey's Christmastime Ball* stage show includes Disney characters singing and dancing, and the *Magical Frozen Snowfall* ceremony welcomes Anna from Frozen with dancers and music.

The tree-lighting ceremony happens every evening and is an unmissable ceremony when the park's huge Christmas tree lights up.

Finally, there are plenty of limited-edition merchandise and food and drink offerings.

The Future – Projects in Progress

Hong Kong Disneyland has expanded greatly in the last 15 years, and the next few years are set to continue to be exciting as more experiences are added to the park.

This year, in 2020, *Sleeping Beauty Castle* will finish its two-year-long transformation into the *Castle of Magical Dreams*. This new-look castle will be accompanied by a new nighttime spectacular and viewing area.

2021 is the expected opening year for *Arendelle: World of Frozen*, an entirely new land themed to the Frozen films. The land will feature a clone of the boat ride from Walt Disney

World's Epcot called *Frozen Ever After*, as well as a new family roller coaster called *Wandering Oaken's Sliding Sleighs* which will work similarly to *Seven Dwarves Mine Train* seen at Walt Disney World and Shanghai Disney Resort.

In 2023, a new Marvel-themed attraction will arrive completing The Avengers Campus, *Avengers Quinjet,* where you will fly alongside the Avengers using an all-new ride system.

A Special Thanks

Thank you very much for reading our travel guide. We hope this book has made a big difference to your trip to Hong Kong Disneyland, and that you have found some tips that will save you time, money and hassle! Remember to take this guide with you when you are visiting the resort. This guide is also available in a digital format.

If you have any feedback about any element of the guide, or have noticed changes in the parks that differ from what is in the book, do let us know by sending us a message. To contact us, visit our website at www.independentguidebooks.com.

If you enjoyed the guide, we would love for you to leave a review on Amazon or wherever you have purchased this guide. Your reviews make a huge difference in helping other people find this guide. Thank you.

Have a magical time!

If you have enjoyed this guide, other travel guides in this series include:
• The Independent Guide to Tokyo Disney Resort
• The Independent Guide to Shanghai Disney Resort
• The Independent Guide to Disneyland Paris
• The Independent Guide to Universal Orlando
• The Independent Guide to Universal Studios Hollywood
• The Independent Guide to Walt Disney World
• The Independent Guide to Disneyland
• The Independent Guide to Hong Kong
• The Independent Guide to Tokyo
• The Independent Guide to Dubai
• The Independent Guide to Paris
• The Independent Guide to London
• The Independent Guide to New York City

Coming later in 2020 is a new guide to Universal Studios Japan too.

Photo credits:

The following photos in this guide have been used from Flickr (unless otherwise stated) under a Creative Commons license. Thank you to: Hollywood Hotel – Martin Lewison; Fastpass ticket – Joel ('coconut wireless').

Some images are copyright The Walt Disney Company and Hong Kong Disneyland.

Hong Kong Disneyland Map

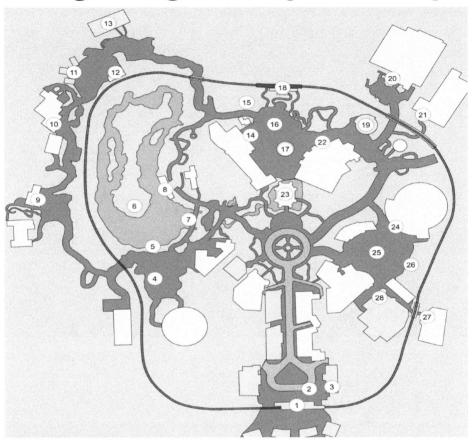

MAIN STREET, U.S.A.
1 - Hong Kong Disneyland Railroad - Main street Station
2 - Main Street Vehicles
3 - Animation Academy

ADVENTURELAND
4 - Festival of the Lion King
5 - Rafts to Tarzan's Treehouse
6 - Tarzan's Treehouse
7 - Moana: A Homecoming Celebration
8 - Jungle River Cruise

GRIZZLY GULCH
9 - Big Grizzly Mountain Runaway Mine Cars

MYSTIC POINT
10 - Mystic Manor

TOY STORY LAND
11 - Toy Soldier Parachute Drop

12 - Slinky Dog Spin
13 - RC Racer

FANTASYLAND
14 - Mickey's Philharmagic
15 - Fairy Tale Forest
16 - Dumbo the Flying Elephant
17 - Cinderella Carousel
18 - Hong Kong Disneyland Railroad - Fantasyland Station
19 - Mad Hatter Tea Cup
20 - "it's a small world"
21 - Mickey and the Wondrous Book
22 - The Many Adventures of Winnie the Pooh
23 - Castle of Magical Dreams

TOMORROWLAND
24 - Hyperspace Mountain
25 - Orbitron
26 - Jedi Training: Trials of the Temple
27 - Iron Man Experience
28 - Ant-Man and The Wasp: Nano Battle

Printed in the USA
CPSIA information can be obtained
at www.ICGtesting.com
LVHW051206150224
771942LV00003B/752